Business

C**h**ec**k**lists

O

&

Ma

Hodder & Stoughton

A MEMBER OF THE HODDER HEADLINE GROUP

Orders; please contact Bookpoint Ltd, 78 Milton Park, Abingdon, Oxon OX14 4TD.
Telephone: (44) 01235 400414, Fax: (44) 01235 400454. Lines are open from 9.00–6.00,
Monday to Saturday, with a 24 hour message answering service.
Email address: orders@bookpoint.co.uk

British Library Cataloguing in Publication Data
A catalogue record for this title is available from the British Library

ISBN 0 340 74291 7

First published 1999
Impression number   10 9 8 7 6 5 4 3 2 1
Year   2005 2004 2003 2002 2001 2000 1999

Copyright © 1999 Institute of Management

Typeset by GreenGate Publishing Services, Tonbridge, Kent.
Printed in Great Britain for Hodder and Stoughton Educational, a division of Hodder
Headline Plc, 338 Euston Road, London NW1 3BH, by Redwood Books, Trowbridge,
Wiltshire

2183

Contents

in the Institute of Management

F O U N D A T I O N

The mission of the Institute of Management (IM) is to promote the art and science of management.

The Institue embraces all levels of management from student to chief executive and supports its own Foundation which provides a unique portfolio of services for all managers, enabling them to develop skills and achieve management excellence.

For information on the various levels and benefits of membership, please contact:

Department HS

Institute of Management

Cottingham Road

Corby

Northants NN17 1TT

Tel: 01536 204222

Fax: 01536 201651

Preface

The first Business Checklists were launched by the Institute of Management in 1995. They met with immediate success from managers in all sectors of commerce and industry, and in organisations of all shapes and sizes.

They originated from one simple idea – that managers did not have the time, or indeed the inclination, to plough through heavy tomes of turgid prose in order to unearth the odd nugget or two which might enable them to do their jobs a little better. They also drew their origins from a former series of Checklists by the British Institute of Management which had been successful in the 1970s.

So why are they so successful? Basically because they cut out unnecessary waffle. They express in clear, concise language what managers need to know, and are presented in a consistent format so that it is easy to pick out the bits you want. They have a wide application, outside business as well as inside, and in small or large organisations: introducing a concept or technique, explaining the pros and cons, dos and don'ts, and steps to follow to get you started. They also provide further pointers for those who do have the time, inclination or need to pursue the topic in greater depth.

Updated and revised since their launch, the Business Checklists are here presented for the first time in a series of books which bring them together under broad management functions.

How are the subjects chosen? Not by guesswork or experts who think they know best, but by demand. The Institute's Management Information Centre handles over 50,000 enquiries a year so the Centre's researchers not only have a good idea of what managers are looking for but also how they want it delivered.

Each checklist follows a similar pattern:

MCI Standards

The MCI Management Standards are the underpinning structure for many vocational management qualifications. Each checklist identifies the appropriate subject content of the standards that it meets.

Definition

Clarifies the coverage of the checklist, highlighting both what is and what is not included in its scope.

Advantages and disadvantages

Each checklist highlights the benefits and pitfalls of the topic, providing a quick insight into the experiences of others.

Action checklist

The core of the checklist is the step-by-step sequence, written in jargon-free language and designed to help readers get to grips with a task quickly.

Dos and don'ts

A brief summary of the key items to remember – and to avoid – on each topic.

Useful reading and organisations

Sources of additional information for readers wishing to investigate the topic further.

Thought starters

Some introductory ideas to help readers begin to approach the subject in a practical way.

Although the Business Checklists constitute a wide-ranging, but concise, library of management know-how, we don't pretend – yet – that they are complete. As they are being continually updated and revised, please get in touch with the Institute of Management's Information Centre in Corby if you have suggestions for future editions.

Bob Norton
Head of Information Services
Institute of Management.

Setting Objectives

This checklist is designed for those managers who participate in setting corporate objectives and who then have to interpret and apply such objectives to their own functional or departmental operation, including setting objectives with and for the people under their responsibility.

MCI Standards

This checklist has relevance for the MCI Management Standards: Key Roles A, C and G – Manage Activities, Manage People and Manage Projects.

Definition

An objective is an end towards which effort is directed and on which resources are focused. An objective should be specific (so that it is clear to those who are to work towards it), measurable (so that people will know when they have got there or not), and usually tackled within certain time and cost constraints.

Setting corporate objectives means clarifying the strategic and policy requirements of the organisation and setting and agreeing complementary operational objectives in relation to them. It is an integrated process which links corporate planning to business operations. As objectives are 'rolled down' the organisation, they are usually made more specific. Every department, every team and every individual can and should have objectives.

Much ink has been spilled over the differences between aims, objectives, goals and targets. There are no real differences except those of scale and time; some may be long-term and high-level, others short-term and low-level. The key is to use the terms that you – and the people you are dealing with – understand. Throughout this checklist we use the term objective.

Requirements of objectives

In order to have a chance of success, objectives need to:

- identify a purpose and an area of responsibility such as improving performance or service
- be specific and measurable
- be achievable but challenging – within given time and resources

- be written down – for both clarification and referral
- be subjected to a process of discussion, compromise and agreement between those setting the objective and those who are to tackle it
- be agreed with the performer – this is not always possible but highly desirable because ownership leads to commitment.

Advantages of integrated objective-setting

These include:

- a better understanding of corporate planning at operational level
- a clear sense of direction
- a better understanding of accountability throughout the organisation
- greater understanding in setting priorities
- improved communication and motivation.

Managing without objectives

By failing to manage by objectives you risk:

- not knowing where you are going
- never knowing what you have achieved
- not knowing whether what you are doing is in tune with longer-term plans or higher-level objectives
- confusion and demoralisation.

Action Checklist

1. Develop and communicate the organisation's Mission/Vision statements

People often confuse a Mission with a Vision statement. It is quite possible – even desirable – to have objectives relating to both.

The Mission statement lays down the purpose for which the organisation exists and provides the umbrella statement for the organisation's 'standing' objectives.

The Vision statement is the expression of an ultimate aim to which the organisation aspires and encapsulates the 'change' objectives.

For example:

- Our purpose is to make top quality cars. (Mission)
- Our aim is to become the largest-selling car manufacturer in the world by the year 2005. (Vision)

Such statements should be clearly communicated to and reinforced with all personnel, not just senior management.

2. Identify corporate objectives from the Mission/Vision statement

It is important to link corporate objectives to Mission and Vision statements. This is usually the purpose of the strategic plan and the function of senior management, although this process is being increasingly cascaded throughout the organisation in empowered organisations.

The strategic plan is formulated by an assessment of:

- what the organisation intends to accomplish and where it intends to be in terms of its market position vis-a-vis the competition
- being in the right markets at the right time with the right product(s) and service(s)
- ensuring a sustainable and profitable growth.

Much will depend on the values of the organisation; values may well be challenged and re-assessed when setting high-level objectives, and vice versa – the adoption of new objectives may well lead to a reappraisal of values. The organisation's values will influence how it tackles its objectives in terms of the importance it attaches to the environment, the welfare of its staff and job security, and its public image in general.

For many organisations however, objective-setting still remains a largely top-down exercise. In such cases, objectives should be set out in a plan and communicated to all staff.

3. Agree the objectives for senior managers

This is a process of splitting the corporate objectives by function, business unit, or by product or service. It will be necessary to rank the objectives in terms of priority, draw up time-frames for achieving them and identify the resources required to tackle them: this precedes the operational and financial (budgeting) planning of that function or business unit.

4. Cascade to departments and individuals

Again, some organisations make this a two-way process so that communication on key decisions is bottom-up as well as top-down. Don't wait forever for top-down objectives; establish your own at departmental level which reflect the organisation's mission, and are in harmony with what your customers need and what your resources are geared to deliver.

5. Agree objectives with those who are to tackle them

Setting objectives should not happen by dictat or decree; rather it should be by proposing and seeking ideas, by discussion, negotiation, compromise and agreement. That is an ideal situation; the minimum that both objective-setter and objective-performer should require from a one-to-one meeting is an answer to each of Kipling's six honest serving-men: who, what, where, when, why and how?

6. Identify appropriate performance measures

Performance measures should allow progress against objectives to be measured.

Performance measures (which can be employed on a team or individual basis) should indicate what is expected and how well people are doing towards their objectives. Performance measures should be clear, concise, easy to collect and interpret, and relevant in that they should provide information which tells you and your organisation how well you are performing.

Measures are usually related to:

- efficiency (how quickly you deliver)
- effectiveness (how good/accurate/relevant was the service delivery for the customer)
- cost-efficiency
- cost-effectiveness.

They would usually cover information relating to:

- finance – costs as well as income
- customers – new and lost
- markets – penetration thereof
- resources – consumed, saved or required anew
- processes – how efficiently and effectively, tasks and activities are accomplished.

Performance measures should also be agreed between job holder and manager and should be reviewed regularly (especially if there are significant changes to the work content). They are of benefit to the organisation or the individual in terms of personal development. Managers may well need time to help staff understand and interpret objectives for their department or their part of the organisation, even to help them work out their own contribution to corporate objectives. (Performance measures are the subject of a further checklist Establishing a Performance Measurement System beginning on page 6).

This – with section 6 above – is the principal content of the performance appraisal. It is in the appraisal discussion that past performance is reviewed, learning opportunities are identified and new or revised objectives are set for the next period.

Dos and don'ts in objective setting

Do

- Set priorities by ranking that which 'must' be done and that which 'we would like to have done'.
- Write objective statements which are SMART – Specific, Measurable, Action-oriented, Realistic, Time (and resource) constrained.

Don't

- Leave out those who are responsible for achieving the goal from the discussion and agreement process necessary to setting it.
- Neglect to re-start the cycle by reviewing and revising objectives.

Further reading

Performance management textbook, Jeff Coates ed., London: CIMA, 1997

The performance management handbook, Mike Walters, London: Institute of Personnel and Development, 1995

Managing for high performance: a practical guide, Roger Moores, London: Industrial Society, 1994

From corporate to individual: the objectives cascade, Chartered Institute of Management Accountants, London: CIMA, 1994

Goals and goal setting: planning to succeed, Larrie A Rouillard, London: Kogan Page, 1993

Thought starters

- Are you clear on the 'fit' between what you do and where the organisation is going?
- Do your people have clear targets which are live issues in the work-place?
- Are targets measured for performance against financial, customer and personal development indicators?

Establishing a Performance Measurement System

This checklist provides guidance on establishing a performance measurement system for an organisation or department.

The primary purpose of performance measurement is to measure how well an organisation or department is accomplishing its mission, goals or objectives. Measuring performance is one of the key requisites in any continuous improvement programme. The information gained from performance measures may be used to establish a programme to benchmark against competitors, other organisations or previous results.

MCI Standards

This checklist has relevance for the MCI Management Standards: Key Role A – Manage Activities.

Definition

A performance measurement system provides an organised means of defining, collecting, analysing, and making decisions regarding all performance measures within a process or activity.

A *performance indicator* is a level against which the management of any activity can be assessed. Measurement against the indicator enables managers to assess how efficiently, effectively and cost-effectively the operation is performing.

Performance measures provide a quantitative answer to whether you are reaching or exceeding the indicator set. They require the collection of raw data and conversion through a formula into a numerical unit.

For example a target may have been set to reduce the number of customer complaints from 10% of total sales to 5% (the indicator). A formula to see whether this has been achieved would look like this:

$$\frac{\text{total number of complaints}}{\text{total number of sales}} \times 100 \ = \ \% \text{ of complaints}$$

Advantages of measuring performance

Measuring performance enables an organisation to:

- understand its current position
- determine whether improvements have actually taken place
- ascertain where improvements need to be made
- understand its processes more clearly
- ensure decisions are made on the basis of fact
- identify whether or not it is meeting its targets.

Disadvantages of measuring performance

The only drawback may be in terms of the resources (staff and time) that measuring performance consumes. This should not be underestimated if a performance measurement system is to be introduced. Introduction should also clarify that it is a process or activity which is to be measured, not the person.

Action checklist

1. Designate a Performance Measurement System Committee

The members of the Performance Measurement System Committee (PMSC) should be drawn from all levels of the organisation. The PMSC will be responsible for the design, implementation and review of the performance measurement system. Appoint a coordinator (someone with project management experience who commands respect and can get things done) to oversee the system. By including members from all levels of the organisation the whole process, from beginning to end, can be mapped.

2. Identify the process that you wish to measure

Examples of processes in practice include purchasing new materials, getting the finished product ready for delivery, invoicing, and handling complaints. Usually each will need its own performance indicators and measures. Questions the PMSC should consider when defining the processes for their organisation are:

- what product or service do we produce?
- who are our customers (internal and external)?
- what comprises our processes?

- what do we do?
- how do we do it?
- what starts and what ends our process?

The processes should be clearly defined, and a flow chart should be produced to increase clarity.

3. Identify the activities to be measured

By examining the process flow chart the PMSC will be able to identify activities that are critical in terms of:

- total process efficiency and cost-efficiency
- total process effectiveness and cost-effectiveness
- total process quality, zero defects or customer satisfaction
- total process timeliness
- total process productivity
- total process safety.

Critical activities will be those:

- that have to be watched closely and acted on if their performance is less than specified
- that should be continuously improved
- whose benefits exceed the cost of taking the measurement.

Once these activities have been defined it is necessary to identify what useful information is required from each activity to be measured.

4. Establish performance indicators

For each of the critical activities selected for measurement, it is necessary to establish a performance indicator. Remember there may, in some cases, be legislative standards to meet, for example in the area of toxic emissions.

Good performance indicators are:

- realistic – they do not require unreasonable effort to meet
- understandable – they should be expressed in simple and clear terms
- adaptable – they can be changed if conditions change
- economic – the cost of setting and administering should be low in relation to the activity covered
- legitimate – they should at least meet legislative requirements
- measurable – they should be communicable with precision.

A period of observation may be appropriate if it is the first time an indicator is to be established for an activity. Additionally, similar organisations to your own may be prepared to offer information on the targets they set – this can then be used to establish indicators of your own. From the performance indicator you will be able to identify what data needs to be collected.

5. Collect the data

To determine how the data will be collected ask yourself:

- what am I trying to measure?
- where will I make the measurement?
- how accurate and precise must the measurements be?
- how often do I need to take the measurement?

For activities that are undertaken a number of times an hour it may be feasible for only a sample measure to be taken, say every eighth event.

In many cases the data required for the performance measurement will already exist, for example in databases, log books, time cards, and checksheets. If additional data is required it will usually be the responsibility of the person in charge of that particular area of the activity to collect it.

Remember, there will be some instances where an automated data collection system can or should be installed to provide accurate data without the need for human intervention.

Inform the relevant individuals of when they should start collecting data and in what format the data should be presented, ie datasheets or in spreadsheet format. All the data should be passed on to a member of the PMSC for analysis.

6. Analyse/report actual performance

Before drawing conclusions from the data, verify that:

- the data appear to answer the questions that were originally asked
- there is no evidence of bias in the collection process
- there are enough data to draw meaningful conclusions.

Once the data have been verified the required performance measurement can be formulated. This may involve the use of a computer spreadsheet if there is a large amount of data.

Summarise the data and prepare a report. Follow these concepts:

- categorise the data and use graphs to show trends
- make the report comparative to goals or standards
- ensure all performance measurements start and end on the same month or year
- adopt a standard format by using the same size sheets and charts
- add basic conclusions.

7. Compare actual performance to indicators

The results of the performance measures should be compared to the indicator set for each activity. A further report may be needed to present to senior management for action.

8. Make modifications to the activity

Once the indicators have been analysed the following may be seen:

- the activity is under-performing – the indicator should be left as it is, but reasons for failure should be identified and action to remedy failure should be taken
- variance is not significant – a higher indicator should be set to achieve continuous improvement
- the indicator is easily achieved – if indicators are not challenging, then continuous improvement is unlikely to be encouraged. Indicators should be reviewed and raised.

9. Continue measuring performance and evaluating the performance measures

The whole process of collecting data and analysing performance should be continued. Remember that goals and standards should be increased as performance improves, or changed as activities change. For example, the purchase of new plant may mean that a component can be produced more quickly and efficiently than before.

Dos and don'ts of measuring performance

Do
- Measure only what is important.
- Involve staff who are part of the activity to be measured from the outset.
- Review the indicators on a regular basis to enable continuous improvement.

Don't
- Set performance measures in stone – modify them as processes and activities change.
- Forget to act on the results of the performance measurement system.
- Be surprised if indicators are not met immediately – performance measurement should be used to drive continuous improvement.

Useful reading

BOOKS

Performance measurement in service industries: making it work, Lin Fitzgerald and Philip Moon, London: CIMA, 1996

Developing comprehensive performance indicators, Ontario: Society of Management Accountants of Canada, 1994

Measuring performance for business results, Mohamed Zairi, London: Chapman and Hall, 1994

JOURNAL ARTICLES

A measured approach, Richard Anderson, Best Practice UK, November 1996, pp13–18

Measuring your way to profit, Umit S Bititci, Management Decision, vol 32 no 6, 1994, pp16–24

Thought starters

- How did any organisation that you have previously worked for measure their performance?
- What are your organisation's / department's key activities?
- How can you manage what you can't measure?

Implementing an Effective Change Programme

> This checklist is intended for those who have mapped a change programme for the organisation and are now ready to implement it. It provides pointers to the issues you will need to consider in bringing in change, rather than providing a detailed implementation schedule: this will vary according to the organisation and the nature of the change.

MCI standards

This checklist has relevance for the MCI Management Standards: Key Roles A and G – Manage Activities and Manage Projects.

Definition

This checklist covers any type of major change programme within an organisation. These range from those driven by external forces – changes in the market; in customer demands; in legislation or regulation – to those which are internally driven, for example, to accompany a total quality management programme.

Change will result as a consequence of the interaction between equipment (technology), processes (working procedures), organisation structure and people; a change to one of these four elements will inevitably cause changes to the others, because the organisation is a living, evolving system.

Managing change involves accomplishing a transition from A to B and handling the problems which arise in getting there.

Action checklist

1. Agree the implementation strategy

The details of the strategy need to be clear before you begin to embark on change. Is implementation going to be top-down or bottom-up or a mix of both? Will the change be made by division, by department or in a 'big bang' approach?

2. Agree the time frame

Every change programme needs a start date and a finite time span, regardless of whether it is being introduced incrementally or simultaneously across divisions. The time table must be stretching enough to convey urgency but attainable enough to be motivating.

3. Draw up detailed implementation plans

Combine the strategy and timetable to draw up detailed implementation plans with each divisional or departmental head. Use the change team as a source of advice and consultancy, but empower line managers to determine how they will implement the details of change against the overall goals.

The change programme is unlikely to be the only corporate initiative underway. Ensure the strategy and goals behind the others are consistent and point in the same direction. Do employees receive consistent messages about the organisation's core values and beliefs from each of the programmes?

4. Set up a team of stakeholders

This does not include top management but will benefit from top management sponsorship. The team will include the key people involved in designing and delivering the service as well as those receiving it. They will also be responsible for defining and disseminating the benefits of the change.

5. Establish good project management

Treat change like any project. Set goals and milestones and monitor progress to keep the project on schedule and on budget. Flag up potential problems as early as possible and plan for them with contingencies. Establish the project team ground-rules especially on information sharing, decision-making and reporting.

6. Personalise the case for change

People will only take on board the case for change when they can personalise it and relate it to their own job and team. Ensure that your line managers translate the corporate case for change into reality for every individual in the company. Consider what change will mean for each individual in terms of: status (job title, budget responsibility); habits (changes to working time, new colleagues); beliefs (move to a customer focus); and behaviour (new working practices).

7. Ensure participation

Individual employees must feel they can take ownership of the change programme as it evolves. Change can be stressful if imposed. Introduce mechanisms to facilitate this. Allow criticism and feedback but ensure the means exist to take corrective action.

8. Create a sense of purpose and urgency to tackle real problems, which have prevented progress in the past

Ask what and who is preventing progress and who can really help in unblocking it.

Think of breaking the code of silence that engenders organisational protectionism and maintains the status quo.

9. Motivate

Sustained change requires very high levels of motivation. People need to feel valued, to be developed, to have their achievements recognised, and to be challenged. Recognise that different rewards will motivate different people to change.

10. Be prepared for conflict

Change usually brings about conflict of one kind or another, simply because people have different views and reactions. Try to get conflict to surface rather than fester; try to tackle it by dissecting and analysing it with those who are experiencing it. Often enough conflict can be put to positive work through open discussion and clarification.

11. Be willing to negotiate

When conflict cannot be resolved through improved explanation and discussion, you will have to negotiate and persuade. This means avoiding entrenched positions, and working out how to shift others from theirs. It means getting to an agreed 'yes' without either side winning or losing face.

12. Anticipate stress

It is uncertainty rather than change that really worries employees. Provide as much information as possible and quash rumours as soon as they arise.

Any change programme is stressful. Fear of the unknown rather than change itself is the major contributory factor. Reduce its impact by being as open as possible about all the consequences of change. See that employees own the changes.

13. Build skills

View the change programme as a learning process and integrate it into the corporate training programme. Build both technical and soft skills at all levels within the organisation. Set an example by updating the skills of top management.

14. Build in capability for learning

Creating goals and plans that everyone subscribes to means that everyone can gain. Turn learning into something that people want to buy into – instead of it being perceived as a chore – where they can feel the 'buzz' of discovery and involvement in new developments.

15. Remember change is discontinuous

Change is a very long process made up of very small and often invisible modifications to behaviour and attitudes. Seek innovative ways to remind staff of the overall case for change and to reinforce its value to them.

Accept that change will be a stop/start process. Plan for this and develop strategies to gear the organisation up for renewed effort if there are setbacks.

16. Monitor and evaluate

Monitor and evaluate the results of the change programme against the goals and milestones established in the original plan. Are these goals still appropriate or do they need to be revised in the light of experience?

Existing performance measures may transmit the wrong signals and act as a block on change. Design measures which are consistent with the vision and goals.

Be honest in your assessment of progress. If there is a real divergence between the plan goals and reality take corrective action quickly. Be open about failure and involve employees in setting new targets or devising new measures.

Dos and don'ts for effective change

Do

- Plan to deliver early tangible results and publicise successes to build momentum and support.
- Select priorities for change rather than attempt to address everything at once.
- Involve employees at every stage of designing and implementing change.
- Make sure you have top management sponsorship of and commitment to the agreed implementation.

Don't

- Fail to appreciate the depth of resistance there may be to change. Plan for resistance and cost it in terms of additional training and communications.
- Get lost in detail or lose sight of the vision: real change often comes through a simple breakthrough.
- Skimp on the resources for training or communications.

Useful reading

How to be better at managing change, D E Hussey, London: Kogan Page, 1998

Create that change: readymade tools for change management, Steve Smith, ed., London: Kogan Page, 1997

A real life guide to organizational change, George Blair and Sandy Meadows, Aldershot: Gower, 1996

Better change: best practices for transforming your organisation, Price Waterhouse Change Integration Team, New York: Irwin Professional Publishing, 1995

A manual for change, Terry Wilson, Aldershot: Gower, 1994

A force for change: how leadership differs from management, John P Kotter, New York: Free Press, 1990

The change masters: corporate entrepreneurs at work, Rosabeth Moss Kanter, London: Unwin Paperbacks, 1988

Thought starters

- Which indicators will tell you if change has really been effected?
- What signals should top management send to employees to show the extent of their commitment to change?
- What messages will indicate successful staff ownership of change?

Implementing Business Process Re-Engineering

This checklist provides an outline guide, as a synthesis of best practice, to the key stages in implementing Business Process Re-engineering (BPR).

BPR is multi-faceted. At its centre are two distinctive aspects: the understanding that organisations are process-driven (not function-driven); and an appreciation of the far-reaching, quantum leap approach encouraged by BPR.

BPR has many characteristics in common with Total Quality Management (TQM): both require extensive commitment from staff and rely heavily on teamwork and problem-solving to improve businesses processes in pursuit of customer satisfaction. But BPR also differs from TQM in that its essence lies in discontinuous thinking, and in rejecting the assumptions, received wisdom and routine thinking that frame the way of doing things in many businesses. In this respect it is similar to strategic benchmarking, being based on the principle that the critical review of internal processes can reveal 'break points' towards significant improvements in quality and competitiveness.

MCI standards

This checklist has relevance for the MCI Management Standards: Key Roles A and B – Manage Activities and Manage Resources.

Definition

'Re-engineering' is a way to initiate and to control change processes through imaginative analysis and systematic planning.

Any organisation (regardless of size, type or desired objective) operates fundamentally by transforming a collection of 'inputs' (for example, raw materials or raw data) into required 'outputs' (for example, products or services). This transformation involves one or more processes. In order to gain competitive advantage, an organisation must transform inputs into outputs more efficiently than its competitors by concentrating on the efficiency of these core processes. This requires regular review and improvement of the relevant processes. Hammer and Champy define BPR as:

'The fundamental rethinking and radical design of business processes to achieve dramatic improvements in critical contemporary measures of performance, such as cost, quality, service and speed.'

The improvements in process quality to be gained from BPR lie in three dimensions – process efficiency (eg cost, cycle time), product quality (eg customer satisfaction, scope and quality of product) and product development time.

Advantages of BPR

- BPR often creates new markets through the identification of 'break points'.
- BPR encourages creativity and innovation in teams.

Disadvantages of BPR

- BPR suits products and services that involve logical sequences in production. It may be less suitable for highly variable processes.
- BPR initiatives often require a high investment in IT.
- The high cost of BPR initiatives can speed up the collapse of companies already in trouble.
- BPR requires good teamwork and a high level of expertise.
- The creation of a lean organisation through 'down-sizing' may actually reduce its capacity to change.

Action checklist

1. Develop the vision – think big

Senior management needs to gain a perception of the problems in the current business. An awareness of customer expectations, competitors' advantage and opportunities resulting from IT lead this process.

Create a clear grand vision. Thinking big and bold is the essence of BPR.

2. Establish a steering committee

Membership should be cross-functional. Specialists and consultants may be included, but a balance needs to be maintained. Senior managers must lead the project and provide strategic direction. The committee needs to understand the key leverage points in the organisation. At an early stage it will need to decide whether it is going to undertake a pilot programme or go for an all-embracing project.

The committee should outline a preliminary strategy and set goals for the organisation. Use appropriate survey techniques to listen to the customer, benchmark the competition and analyse existing processes. Identify where there is a gap between performance and customer expectations.

3. Prepare the organisation for change

Communication is the key to success with change. Promote a sense of urgency. Present the business case for change, highlighting the objectives and goals of re-engineering. Encourage feedback and input from all employees.

4. Analyse existing processes

Model current processes in detail. Re-affirm which processes need to exist and why. This reduces the likelihood of past mistakes being repeated. Listen to the process owners to identify where problems exist. Document each and every helpful idea and ensure these are widely circulated. Focus the redesign on those points which can provide the greatest return.

5. Establish performance indicators or baselines

Improvements in performance can only be identified if you know where you are starting from. Performance measures include:

- transaction volumes
- cycle times
- defect rates
- customer satisfaction levels.

Make sure that the three dimensions of process efficiency, product quality and product development time are examined comprehensively. The approach adopted in strategic benchmarking can prove useful in identifying potential 'break points' for future success.

6. Redesign the process

Start with the needs of the customer and re-design the process from outside-in. Apply the following guidelines to the redesign process:

- Collect information that is required throughout the life-cycle of the process only once, at its point of origin, and make it available immediately to all who need it.
- Reduce the need for coordination by associating individuals with processes, not with departments or functions.
- Improve customer service through genuine empowerment, trust and delegation of responsibility, allowing partnerships to develop with customers and suppliers.

- Identify the key business outcomes, the business processes required to produce such outcomes and descriptions of how processes interrelate. It will also be necessary to lay out the infrastructure required to support the change by describing the:
  - management strategy, measurement systems and reward programmes
  - organisational values and individual belief systems that need to be adopted by all concerned.

7. Plan the implementation

Once a process has been redesigned an implementation plan can be prepared. Changes need time to implement, so, although BPR aims to achieve dramatic improvement in a short time, the planned schedule of change should not be unrealistically short.

Re-emphasise the need for change and communicate the vision to managers and employees to overcome the natural uncertainty that exists. Gain approval and popular support by outlining the expected benefits to be achieved by the proposed redesign.

An implementation plan should take into account that:

- schedules, budgets, completion criteria and economic justifications all need to be specified
- training will be vital to smooth the transition
- new control systems need to be established
- immediate feedback on improvements is essential
- contingencies are needed to allow for problems which will inevitably occur
- changes in physical location or layout, work flows and organisation structures, plant and IT systems, testing and pilot projects and a redefinition of roles and responsibilities will result from the process
- the plan should deliver some significant but quick results in the early stages to build commitment.

8. Monitor and evaluate progress

Monitor the process continually to ensure that the expected benefits are being obtained. Feed back results to employees to let everyone gain by knowing what has, and has not worked. This should encourage them, and also in turn help to identify further areas for improvement.

Dos and don'ts for BPR

Do

- Question all assumptions. Identify the organisation's 'sacred cows' and study them carefully.
- Choose your consultants carefully.

Don't

- Assume you are on the right BPR track merely by introducing the latest IT.
- Just settle for automating existing processes.
- Focus on individual tasks at the expense of the overall process.
- Embark on grand projects without resources and support to complete them.
- Confuse BPR with rationalisation.

Useful reading

BOOKS

Reengineering the corporation, Michael Hammer and James Champy, London: Nicholas Brealey Publishing, 1993

Business reengineering: the survival guide, Dorine C Andrews and Susan K Stalick, Eaglewood Cliffs NJ: Prentice Hall, 1994

JOURNAL ARTICLES

Reengineering work: don't automate, obliterate, Michael Hammer, Harvard Business Review, vol 90 no 4, July/August, 1990, pp104–112

Business process reengineering: evocation, elucidation and exploration, Chung For Choi and Stephen L Chan, Business Process Management Journal, vol 3 no 1, 1997, pp39–63

Reengineering. A breakthrough or little new? Sumer Aggarwal, International Journal of Technology Management, vol 13 no 3, 1997, pp326–344

Thought starters

- Do you know what proportion of resources is spent on the core processes in your organisation?
- 60% of BPR initiatives result in little or no gain – the chief causes of failure are the poor selection of consultants and inadequate commitment from the senior management team.
- If you are considering BPR, examine your reasons very carefully – they will probably indicate your probable success.

Implementing Business Process Re-Engineering

A Programme for Benchmarking

This checklist is for managers new to benchmarking or for those wishing to review their current benchmarking practice.

Benchmarking is a powerful tool for organisations seeking continuous improvement. It is an essential part of many change programmes, including total quality management and business process re-engineering. It is a challenging technique to use and requires careful management and a high level of commitment. Used effectively, it can provide organisations with a continuous competitive advantage.

Various types of benchmarking exist, including:

● **Internal benchmarking** – the measurement and comparison of practices with similar practices in other parts of the organisation.

● **Industry or competitive benchmarking** – industry-specific comparisons made either between direct competitors or from target companies with dissimilar products in the same industry.

● **Functional or non-competitive benchmarking** – the direct comparison of a function in two or more organisations, which may or may not be in the same industry.

● **Generic or best practice/world class benchmarking** – benchmarking of the best practice of recognised world class organisations.

Most organisations can use either one or a mixture of these.

MCI Standards

This checklist has relevance for the MCI Management Standards: Key Roles A and B – Manage Activities and Manage Resources.

Definition

Benchmarking is the ongoing structured process of identifying, understanding and adapting outstanding practices of industry leaders to help an organisation improve its performance and achieve and sustain competitive advantage.

Advantages of benchmarking

- Aids the setting or stretching of performance goals.
- Focuses on and accelerates change.
- Motivates staff by showing what is possible.
- Provides an early warning of competitive disadvantage.

Disadvantages of benchmarking

Benchmarking can fail for a number of reasons, including a lack of commitment, focus or resources. However there are no substantial disadvantages to benchmarking.

Action checklist

1. Plan your study

Identify the critical performance factors at which you wish to excel and from these select the broad areas in which to benchmark. Focus on those activities which are of real importance to your organisation, avoiding the irrelevant, or those activities chosen simply because they are easy to measure.

Select a small number of related processes to benchmark. Do not be too ambitious at this stage, particularly if this is the first benchmarking project your organisation has undertaken. When selecting processes to benchmark remember the critical success factors – benchmarking must have the support of senior management, be part of organisational strategy, and be based upon a sound understanding of your own processes.

Consider the legal and ethical issues of competitive benchmarking. Confidentiality and data security are important issues for benchmarking partners and groups.

2. Identifying personnel

Select a benchmarking team and a team leader. Most benchmarking is done by teams to take advantage of the range of skills and knowledge that they can offer – either use an intact work group, a cross-functional team or a functional team (six members is an average team size). Although much work will be carried out by the benchmarking team, it is advantageous to encourage the participation of all staff, as benchmarking may identify gaps in performance which may require radical change anywhere within the organisation. The involvement of process owners ensures they are part of the evaluation process and can become the champions of change.

3. Examine the process(es) to be benchmarked

Document the process(es) to be benchmarked to gain an understanding of the activities involved. Simple flow charts can be useful aids to help define the inputs to, and outputs from, the process. It is possible that a number of elements could be measured, so it is important for the benchmarking team to determine those which are true indicators of performance.

4. Data collection

Data are required in order to make a comparison between organisations or parts of an organisation. This may be in the form of statistics, ratios or detailed case studies and descriptions. As the key to the success of benchmarking projects the data collection process should be carefully planned. Only collect the data that is required for the decision making process: collecting too much data can be as bad as collecting the wrong data.

5. Identify benchmarking partners

Consider internal sources (different departments, divisions or companies within the organisation) and external partners (competitors, similar industries or best practice/world class performers). Sources that can help in identifying partners include trade and industry journals, market research reports, government studies, databases, suppliers, customers, corporate networks and study tours.

Consider contacting a benchmarking clearing house or a joint interest group. A number of organisations interested in benchmarking are listed under 'Useful addresses'.

Solicit the participation of partners. Organisations are often willing to become involved if they can see that they will also benefit from benchmarking – it should after all be a two-way process. You must be willing to share data and findings as well as respecting confidentiality if requested.

6. Plan and implement the comparison exercise

- Identify the hard and the soft issues which need to be measured. Hard issues include ratios, time and costs. Soft issues might include management style, communications, or customer focus.

- Prepare an action plan. Identify who will collect the data, from where and when. An appropriate survey or interview guide should be developed by the benchmarking team. Questionnaires can be sent by post, completed over the telephone or via site visits. Decide which is the most appropriate for your requirements.

- Collect the data. It is easy to underestimate the time needed to collect the data – err on the side of caution when arranging fact-finding interviews.

7. Collate the data from your organisation and its benchmarking partners.

Draw up a matrix of performance indicators from your benchmarking partners (the use of spreadsheets and databases can help the analysis).

Compare your current performance against the data. Identify where your organisation misses certain elements, fails to match the targets of others and generally needs to improve. The benchmarking team should try to identify the causes of these failures and, with relevant additional staff, plan to remedy them. It is useful to research case studies of best practice, as they can form useful aids to help communicate the objectives of change.

Involve process owners in setting goals to close, meet and exceed the gaps in performance. The benchmarking team should develop detailed action plans, ensuring measures of success are included.

8. Plan and action improvements

Once the business benefits which would result from change have been identified, communicate the benchmarking findings. By demonstrating benefits, support for change will be greater.

Implement the plan, making use of 'process champions' throughout the organisation as catalysts for change. It is at this stage that resources will need to be committed, so it is essential to have senior management support for the project.

9. Monitor and review

Monitor whether the study met its objectives; the impact of the improvements on the organisation; the evidence of a change in the process; the value of the changes to the organisation; the willingness and the barriers to change.

Evaluate the success of the project. Decide if further change is required.

Select the next process to benchmark. Maintaining momentum is one of the most challenging problems in benchmarking.

Dos and don'ts for benchmarking

Do
- Ensure senior management support.
- Ensure that it is a team activity.
- Understand your own processes before starting to look at those of other people.

Don't

- Be too ambitious at the start.
- Underestimate the need for a willingness to change and an openness for new ideas.
- View benchmarking as a tool for providing short term gains.

Useful reading

BOOKS

High performance benchmarking: 20 steps to success, H James Harrington and James S Harrington, New York: McGraw Hill, 1996

The managers guide to benchmarking: essential skills for the new competitive cooperative economy, Jerome P Finnigan, Hemel Hempstead: Jossey Bass, 1996

JOURNAL ARTICLE

Benchmarking your firm's performance with best practice, Stephen Hanman, International Journal of Logistics Management, Vol 8 no 2, 1997, pp1–18

European benchmarking code of conduct, Benchmark, November 1996, pp35–36

How to build a benchmarking team, M J Spendolini, Journal of Business Strategy, Vol 14 no 2, March / April 1993, pp53–57

Useful addresses

Benchmarking Centre, Truscon House, Station Road, Gerrards Cross, Bucks, SL9 8ES, Tel: 01753 890070

Pims Associates, Benchmarking Council, 15 Basinghall Street, London, EC2V 5BR, Tel: 0171 776 2800

Thought starters

- Is the performance of your organisation as good as it could be?
- How do you match up to the performance of competitors?
- Are you focusing purely on financial measures or have you considered all your key processes?
- How do your processes compare with those being run by other organisations?

Implementing the Balanced Scorecard

Traditionally, managers have used a series of indicators to measure how well their organisations are performing. These measures relate essentially to financial issues such as business ratios, productivity, unit costs, growth and profitability. While useful in themselves, they provide only a narrowly focused snapshot of how an organisation performed in the past and give little indication of likely future performance.

During the early 1980s, the rapidly changing business environment prompted managers to take a broader view of performance, and a range of other factors started to be taken into account, exemplified by the McKinsey 7-S model and popularised by In Search of Excellence by Peters and Waterman. These provide a broader assessment of corporate health in both the immediate and longer term. This checklist focuses on the Balanced Scorecard, which was developed by Robert Kaplan and David Norton in the early 1990s with the aim of providing a balanced view of an organisation's performance.

MCI Standards

This checklist has relevance for the MCI Management Standards: Key Role A – Manage Activities.

Definition

The Balanced Scorecard is defined as a strategic management and measurement system that links strategic objectives to comprehensive indicators. The key to the success of the system is that it must be a unified, integrated set of indicators that measure key activities and processes at the core of an organisation's operating environment.

It takes into account not only the traditional 'hard' financial measures but three additional categories of 'soft' quantifiable operational measures. These include:

- **customer perspective** – how an organisation is perceived by its customers
- **internal perspective** – in which issues an organisation must excel

- **innovation and learning perspective** – in which areas an organisation must improve and add value to its products or services or operations.

Measurements taken across these four categories are seen to provide a rounded Balanced Scorecard that reflects organisation performance more accurately and which helps managers to focus on their mission, rather than merely on short-term financial gain. It also helps to motivate staff to achieve the strategic objectives.

Action checklist

Kaplan and Norton have identified a number of stages for the implementation of the Scorecard. These are a mix of planning, interviews, workshops and reviews. The type, size and structure of an organisation will determine the detail of the implementation process and the number of stages adopted.

The main steps include:

1. Preparation

As the Scorecard is inextricably linked to strategy, the first requirement is to clearly define that strategy and ensure that senior staff in particular are familiar with the key issues. Before any other action can be planned, it is essential to have understanding of:

- the strategy
- the key objectives or goals to achieve that strategy
- the three or four critical success factors (CSFs) that are fundamental to the achievement of each major objective or goal.

2. Decide what to measure

Managers should identify the organisation's major strategic goals. As a guide, there should be a total limit of 15 to 20 key measures linked to those specific goals – significantly fewer measures may not achieve a balanced view and significantly more may become unwieldy and deal with non-critical issues.

Based on the four main perspectives suggested by Kaplan and Norton, a list of goals and measures may include some of the following:

Financial (shareholder) perspective
- **Goals** – increased profitability, growth, increased returns on assets.
- **Measures** – cash flows, cost reduction, economic value added, gross margins, profitability, return on capital/equity/investments/sales, revenue growth, working capital, turnover.

Customer perspective

- **Goals** – new customer acquisition, retention, satisfaction.
- **Measures** – market share, customer service, customer satisfaction, number of new/retained/lost customers, customer profitability, number of complaints, delivery times, quality performance, response time.

Internal perspective

- **Goals** – improved core competencies, improved critical technologies, streamlined processes, better employee morale.
- **Measures** – efficiency improvements, development/lead/cycle times, reduced unit costs, reduced waste, amount of recycled waste, improved sourcing/supplier delivery, employee morale and satisfaction, internal audit standards, number of employee suggestions, sales per employee.

Innovation and learning perspective

- **Goals** – new product development, continuous improvement, training of employees.
- **Measures** – number of new products and percentage of sales from these, number of employees receiving training, training hours per employee, number of strategic skills learned, alignment of personal goals with the scorecard.

Each organisation must determine its own strategic goals and activities to be measured. Several organisations have seen Kaplan and Norton's template as not meeting their particular needs and have either modified it or have devised their own Scorecard. Public sector organisations, for example, may have different aims and objectives and may have to tailor the Scorecard to reflect this.

3. Finalise the implementation plan

Further discussions, interviews and workshops may be required to fine-tune the detail, and agree strategy, goals and activities to be measured, ensuring that the measures selected focus on the critical success factors. Other important issues that must be resolved before implementation include setting targets or rates or other criteria for each of the measures, and defining how, when and where they should be recorded.

4. Implement the system

An implementation plan should be produced and the whole project communicated to staff. This should not come as a surprise to anyone, as staff should be informed at the beginning of the project and kept up to date on progress. The way in which the purpose of the Scorecard is communicated is vital. Staff should be made to feel that they have an important part to play in achieving corporate goals. Conversely they should not feel threatened by the measures.

The system for recording and monitoring the metrics should be in place and tested well before the start date, and training in its use should be given to all users as far as possible. The system should automatically record all the data required, though some of the measurements may have to be logged manually.

5. Publicise the results

The results of all measurements should be collated on a regular basis – daily, weekly, monthly, quarterly or as appropriate – and may eventually comprise a substantial amount of possibly complicated data. It will be necessary to decide whether to make the full data available to senior management only, to divisional or departmental heads, or to all staff, or whether to provide partial information on a need-to-know basis. Determine the method of publicising the results – through meetings, newsletters, the organisation's intranet or other means.

6. Utilise the results

Any form of business appraisal is not an end in itself, but is a guide to organisation performance and may point to areas (management, operational, procedural, processural) that require strengthening. Action on the information obtained is as important as the data itself. Indeed, management follow-up action should be seen as an essential part of the process of appraisal.

7. Review and revise the system

After the first cycle has been completed, a review should be undertaken to assess the success or otherwise of the information gathered and action taken, and whether modification is required to any part of the process.

Dos and don'ts for implementing the Balanced Scorecard

Do
- Define your goals clearly.
- Select measures that focus on the critical success factors of each goal.
- Select a manageable number of measures.
- Reassure staff on the purpose of the Scorecard.

Don't
- Over-measure your organisation.
- Allow the measurement process to interfere with employees' ability to get on with the job.
- Adopt an off-the-shelf system not suited to your organisation.

Useful reading

BOOKS

The balanced scorecard: translating strategy into action, Robert S Kaplan and David P Norton, Boston Mass.: Harvard Business School Press, 1996

Performance management textbook, Jeff Coates ed, London: CIMA Publishing, 1997

JOURNAL ARTICLES

Implementing corporate strategy from tableaux de bord to balanced scorecards, Marc Epstein and Jean-Francois Manzoni, European Management Journal, vol 16 no 2, 1998, pp190–203

The new balancing act, Anita van de Vliet, Management Today, July 1997, pp78, 80

Linking the balanced scorecard to strategy, Alan Butler, Steve R Letza and Bill Neale, Long Range Planning, vol 30 no 2, April 1997, pp242–253

Thought starters

- Do you know what measurements are currently taken in your organisation?
- Do the measurements in place give a holistic view of performance?
- Does the organisation try to measure the 'softer' aspects of performance such as learning, innovation and creativity?
- What might be the consequences of not getting a balanced view of your organisation's performance?

Managing Projects

This checklist outlines the steps in project management and provides a framework of sequential action for the manager undertaking a project.

Project management is recognised as a special process which differs in approach from general management or change management. The traditional project management focus has been that of completing defined work within given time constraints and cost limits. Recently the focus has shifted more to the quality of the final output delivered to the customer.

MCI Standards

This checklist has relevance for the MCI Management Standards: Key Role G – Manage Projects.

Definition

'Project management is a specialized management technique to plan and control projects ... A project is generally deemed successful if it meets predetermined targets set by the client, performs the job it was intended to do, or solves an identified problem within the pre-determined time, costs and quality constraints.' – Burke.

Benefits of project management

Project management techniques provide:

- an appropriate way to bring about sudden, revolutionary or purposive change
- a suitable approach for handling one-off tasks
- a realistic method for evaluating a new scheme.

Problems with project management

Projects:

- often require an extraordinary use of resources – especially money and people – over a finite period of time
- usually consume more resources than foreseen
- can go over schedule by significant margins.

Action checklist

1. Define the objectives

Fundamental to the management of any successful project are both understanding and agreement of:

- what is required to be achieved
- what is to be the outcome and/or delivered as a result
- dates and budgets for project completion by both project sponsor and project manager.

Lack of clear objectives will doom the project from the beginning.

2. Appoint the project manager

The project manager must be someone who has a proven track record, can command respect from a mix of seniorities and can get action from them. They should be able to:

- plan and communicate all aspects of the project
- motivate with integrity, sensitivity and imagination
- gain productivity and trust from shared decision-making
- lead both by example and by taking a back seat when appropriate
- monitor costs, efficiency and quality without excessive bureaucracy
- get things done right first time without being a slave-driver
- get the right people for the right task at the right time
- use both technical and general management skills to control the project
- see clear-sightedly through tangled issues.

3. Establish the terms of reference

The terms of reference specify the objectives, scope, time-frames and initial scale of resource required. They should also clarify any risks, constraints or assumptions already identified. It is important to make any early allowances for cost escalation, plans veering off course, and build in a level of contingency, or safety margin.

4. Construct the work breakdown structure document (WBSD)

Having established what the project should achieve, next consider how to achieve it.

The WBSD forms the basis of much subsequent work in planning, setting budgets, exercising control and assigning responsibilities. The key is to break the project down into identifiable phases, then into controllable units for action. Dividing a piece of work into more approachable, discrete units facilitates the functions of estimating, planning and controlling. As soon as possible allocate time-scales to each unit of work, taking care to allow for both sequential units – those that need to be accomplished before the next can be tackled, and overlapping units – those that can run in tandem.

5. Plan for quality

Planning for quality requires both attention to detail and ensuring that the project output or outcome does what it is supposed to, or is 'fit for its purpose'. The work breakdown structure should incorporate 'micro' performance criteria or indicators, for discrete units or phases, and 'macro' indicators against which the final outcome can be assessed. Quality measures (systematic inspections against established standards) should be built into the process from the beginning, not later when things (may) have started to go awry. The formula:

establish standards $\longrightarrow$ monitor performance $\longrightarrow$ take corrective action

can run as a continuous sequence throughout the project duration. The key is to ensure effective quality assurance which acts as a prevention rather than a cure and enables you to get things right first time.

6. Plan costs

A key area in which the most frequent error is to under-estimate costs. Typical cost elements include:

- staff time and wages – usually the most substantial cost item of all
- overheads – employer on-costs
- materials and supplies – the raw materials
- equipment – the pros and cons of leasing or purchasing and the factor of depreciation
- administration – purchasing, accounting, record-keeping.

One of the enabling functions of a good budget is to monitor costs while a project is in progress.

7. Plan time-scales

In order to calculate the shortest time necessary to complete the project you need to know:

- the earliest time a stage or unit can start
- the duration of each stage
- the latest time by which a stage must be completed.

Gantt charts, PERT diagrams and Critical Path Analysis are prominent amongst several project management techniques which can help with effective planning of time-scales.

8. Monitor and report progress

The monitoring of in-progress costs, time-scales and quality is a major factor for consideration throughout the duration of the project. Quality is the hardest to measure and, as such, prone to neglect.

In addition to progress reports, feedback sessions and Management By Walking About, there are various control tools which help check that implementation is going according to plan.

- Control Point Charts ask you what is likely to go wrong in terms of time, cost and quality.
- Project Control Charts provide status reports of actual costs against budget with variances.
- Milestone Charts are a means of showing stages of achievement as steps towards the project objectives.

It is important to know what to do when these, or other, control mechanisms indicate that something is going wrong. Contingency plans are also vital, as goalposts are always prone to movement.

9. Deliver the output

Haynes writes that 'the goal of project management is to obtain client acceptance of the project result'. Steps before delivery of the project outcome may include the compilation of instructional documentation or training packages. The penultimate stage before project completion is ensuring that the outcome of the project is accepted by the customer or sponsor.

10. Evaluate the project

By building in a final stage of evaluation it is possible to gain a measure of the project's success and see what lessons can be learned. Once again, the three key areas for review are quality, time and costs. Others include:

- staff skills gained or identified
- mistakes not to be repeated
- tools and techniques that were valuable
- what would be tackled differently.

Dos and don'ts of project management

Do
- Take time at the beginning on objectives, terms of reference and the work breakdown structure.
- Ensure, as far as possible, access to resources needed.
- Appoint someone with the right skill-mix as project manager.

Don't

- Let small changes creep in without assessing the implications.
- Omit to build in quality checks.
- Lose sight of time targets and budget limits.

Further reading

Successful project management in a week, 2nd ed, Mark Brown, London: Hodder & Stoughton, 1998

Project management, 6th ed, Dennis Lock, Aldershot: Gower, 1996

Project management: strategic design and implementation, 2nd ed, David I Cleland, New York: McGraw Hill, 1994

Project management planning and control, 2nd ed, Rory Burke, Chichester: John Wiley, 1993

Handbook of project-based management: improving the processes for achieving strategic objects, J Rodney Turner, Maidenhead: McGraw Hill, 1992

Some project management software suppliers

Arena Software Ltd, Cambridge, Tel: 01223 464194

Goldcrest Computer Services Ltd, Milton Keynes, Tel: 01908 211330

Microsoft Ltd, Reading, Tel. 0345 002000

PSDI (UK) Ltd, Woking, Tel: 01483 727000

Thought starters

Think of a job or task you have to do.

- Does it have a set start and finish date?
- Does it require a budget?
- Does it need other resources: people, equipment, raw materials?
- Does it involve changing something?
- Does it have a clear objective or target?

Deciding Whether to Outsource

This checklist is for those who must address the decision of whether to outsource or not, and if so, what and how to outsource. The checklist encompasses the stages in the outsourcing process leading up to drawing up and testing a contract.

Seen usually as a threat by employees and an opportunity by organisations, outsourcing is rapidly becoming more accepted. In addition to the inevitable driver of cost-savings, there are many contributory elements which lead an organisation to consider outsourcing, in particular the need for flexibility as demand for products or services rises and falls, and ways of delivering them improve.

On the surface the benefits of outsourcing seem not only straightforward but also considerable. Experience shows, however, that there are many pitfalls, dangers and costs.

MCI standards

This checklist has relevance for the MCI Management Standards: Key Roles B and C – Manage Resources and Manage People.

Definition

Increasingly, outsourcing is understood to mean the retention of responsibility for services by the organisation but devolution of the day-to-day performance of those services to an external organisation, usually under a contract with agreed standards, costs and conditions.

In this checklist the organisation considering outsourcing some or part of its functions will be called the Organisation; the external organisation to take them on will be called the Agency.

Advantages of outsourcing

For the Organisation the decision to outsource takes place for reasons of:

- cost and efficiency savings
- greater financial flexibility through reduced overheads
- operational flexibility and control through contractual relationships
- a wish or a need to focus on core activities
- access to better management skills on non-core activities
- staffing flexibility.

Disadvantages of outsourcing

- Changing support functions may bring about reduced robustness.
- Information flows with the Agency will need careful coordination.
- Reduced learning capacity through a depleted skill-base.
- Declining morale and motivation as jobs appear to 'go'.
- Reduced ability to integrate processes.
- Possible lack of control over activities outsourced.
- Increased insecurity, whether staff remain in the Organisation, or are taken on by the Agency.

Action checklist

1. Establish the outsourcing project team

Treat the outsourcing proposal like a project. Apply the principles of project management, especially selecting a project leader and team, establishing terms of reference, a method of working and an action plan.

2. Analyse your current position

Ideally, you should have carried out a radical review of the organisation's processes – you don't want to outsource an activity that might be better integrated with another you regard as 'core'. Ensure you have assessed:

- the advantage to be achieved by concentration on core services
- minimum involvement required in things that don't affect the customer
- control required of non-diminishing, non-productive overheads
- functions which are more viable through an external agency
- a clear vision of where the business is to be.

3. Pay attention to people

As the contract stage approaches, people will suffer from anxiety and uncertainty. At best their working life will transfer from one employer to another, at worst their job could be lost. Keep people at the forefront of your thinking.

4. Benchmark

Someone, somewhere is probably doing the same thing in a better way, or in the same way at lower cost. Identify appropriate organisations to benchmark against and establish which activities they are outsourcing.

5. Come to a decision

Decide which are your core areas – Tom Peters said: '...do what you do best and outsource the rest'. The principal questions are:

- what is core to the business and to the future of the business?
- what can bring competitive advantage?

Then, decide whether outsourcing should become policy for organisation-wide application to non-core areas or if it is to be used as the need arises.

6. Decide what to outsource

Logically, what to outsource follows from the decision process. If you focus on the core competencies of your organisation, on your uniqueness, then targets for outsourcing become those areas which make up the support, administration, routine and internal servicing of the organisation.

Areas which have traditionally been subject to outsourcing include legal services, transport, catering, printing, advertising, accounting, and, especially, auditing and security. More recently these have been joined by data processing, IT services, information processing, public relations, buildings management and training.

Staff are usually transferred with the function to the Agency. Obviously, this is an area which requires great consideration and sensitivity.

7. Tender the package

The tender is both an objective document detailing the services, activities and targets required, and a selling document which serves to attract those Agencies which can add to the Organisation's capability. Outsourcing is not just a matter of getting rid of problem areas.

Once an attractive package has been defined, send an outline specification and request for information to those Agencies likely to be interested. The outline specification contains the broad intention of the outsourcing proposal and the time-scales the Organisation has in mind. The request for information is a questionnaire-type eligibility test intended to establish the level of the Agency's competence and interest. The second stage is the invitation to tender – a precise document which spells out exactly what Agencies are required to bid for.

8. Choose a partner

The tender process should be used for the evaluation of facts, but choosing an outsourcing partner is much more than choosing a new supplier, because the process involves a customised service, agreement on service levels and a contract. At this stage the Organisation will be looking for an Agency with which it can share objectives and values, have regular senior management meetings, and disclose otherwise confidential information. Harmony of management styles is a key requisite for success. The Organisation will also look for:

- evidence of quality management
- a proven track record, a flexible approach and financial viability
- experience in handling the sensitive issue of staff absorption
- how important in turnover the contract is for the Agency.

9. Meet the staff

It is essential that the Agency meets its prospective new staff before any contracts are signed. Allowing concerns to be aired and questions to be asked may help to reduce feelings of being 'dumped' or cast aside. On the other hand, glaring conflicts in style and personalities may emerge which can have an important impact on the contractual stage. Many other issues involving terms and conditions of employment will need addressing, including those of appropriate compensation if Agency employment is not available or not required.

10. Draw up the contract

If it is to be the project team that draws up the contract it will need to have a strong legal input, especially on TUPE – the Transfer of Undertakings (Protection of Employment) Regulations 1981. Contained within the contract should be:

- minimum service levels that the Agency will provide, and checks and controls that these are met – perhaps via a liaison manager – and clauses including remedies or financial compensation if they are not
- demarcation of service responsibilities and boundaries so that both Organisation and Agency are clear on who is doing what
- who owns what in terms of equipment and hardware
- the fate of the staff to be outsourced and details of their terms and conditions of employment
- flexibility and allowance for change, for example if business volumes double or halve

- a contract term, with a review date and provision for the outsourced function to revert to the Organisation
- a 'what-if' honeymoon period before the contract becomes fully enforced.

11. Test the contract

Ensure that the contract will stand up to the rigours and complexities of the operation in action. A period of testing and trial is ideal for making adjustments before the contract becomes final and to examine the possibility of the partnership breaking down.

Dos and don'ts of outsourcing

Do

- Outsource the 'doing' of an activity, not the responsibility for it.
- Understand the scope of the services to be outsourced.
- Have a clear vision of what outsourcing should achieve.

Don't

- Let the goal of cost savings dominate everything else.
- Think that outsourcing is the answer to all problems.
- Outsource strategic, customer or financial management.

Useful reading

BOOK

The truth about outsourcing, Brian Rothery and Ian Robertson, Aldershot: Gower, 1995

JOURNAL ARTICLES

Do the right thing, John Bell, Business and Technology Magazine, April 1995, pp50–51
Culture, community and networks: the hidden costs of outsourcing, John Hendry, European Management Journal, Vol 13 no 2, June 1995, pp193–200
Outsourcing: making the decision, Malcolm Wheatley, Human Resources UK, January/February 1995, no 16, pp63–64, 66, 68

Useful Organisations

British Institute of Facilities Management, 67 High Street, Saffron Walden, Essex, CB10 1AA, Tel: 01799 508608

Thought starters

- Have you defined the core areas in which you need to excel?
- Do routine and support functions consume an ever larger slice of overheads?
- Can you identify benchmark organisations to track their progress?
- Will outsourcing be an extension of your organisation's operations, or an innovation?

Disaster Planning

This checklist aims to help those putting together a disaster plan for their organisation. It covers physical disasters such as fire, flood, or terrorist attack.

Having a disaster plan means that many decisions are made before the disaster strikes, so that the first crucial days after the disaster are spent on dealing with the situation and not on deciding how to deal with it.

MCI standards

This checklist has relevance for the MCI Management Standards: Key Roles A and B – Manage Activities and Manage Resources.

Definition

A disaster plan (DP) aims firstly to prevent or reduce the likelihood of a disaster by identifying threats and taking the necessary preventative action, and secondly to ensure that the organisation is prepared to deal with an emergency effectively.

Benefits of disaster planning

In the event of a disaster, a DP:

- supports continuity of operations
- mitigates the financial consequences.

Drawbacks of disaster planning

- Poor planning or an out-of-date plan may be worse than no plan at all.
- The planning process can be time-consuming.

Action checklist

1. Establish a disaster planning team

This team should include staff responsible for personnel, buildings, public relations and IT as well as someone with general management responsibility.

You may want to include an external adviser with experience of disaster planning. The appointment of a team leader and a deputy is vital. Senior management should make their commitment to the DP clear to members of the team.

Ensure that the needs of staff and other groups such as customers are taken into account. Identify and prioritise those activities necessary to business continuity – consulting staff throughout the organisation will help to establish a sense of ownership and commitment.

2. Carry out a risk assessment

Identify especially vulnerable aspects of your particular industry, operation or service and determine potential risks, both internal and external, for your organisation. Assess and analyse these and then act to eliminate or reduce them. Distinguish between areas needing immediate action (the repair of broken windows for example) and those which can be dealt with over a longer period (such as the installation of a burglar alarm or sprinkler system). List the extra resources required for these. Consider appointing a loss adjuster in advance so that the insurance claim process can start immediately in the event of a disaster.

Check and seek professional advice where necessary on:

- insurance cover – is the existing cover adequate?
- maintenance of buildings and equipment
- security – do the detection and alarm systems work? If you don't have any, should you consider installing them?
- safety and fire precautions
- storage systems – are important documents held securely? Is adequate off-site storage available for IT back-ups?

3. Draw up a disaster plan

The DP should be simple and easy to understand yet contain all necessary information. It must be developed with the worst case scenario in mind but be flexible enough to be used in less severe cases. Try to obtain examples of other companies' disaster plans and learn from these. Remember that the recovery from the disaster could take twelve months or longer.

The personnel issues to be identified in the DP:

- key personnel – ensure out-of-hours contact details, on a rota basis if necessary, are available
- their responsibilities and limits of authority
- a control centre for the team, preferably off-site.

The DP should contain:

- priorities to be dealt with
- floor plans
- evacuation procedures
- precautionary measures
- details of where further information can be found
- procedures for jobs to be done during the recovery period
- a directory of suppliers, to provide equipment and supplies for use in emergency.

Anticipate the effects on employees, customers, suppliers and others. Consider:

- employees

  - Make sure managers have employees' telephone numbers and addresses at home so that they are able to contact them out of work hours.
  - Be prepared to offer counselling and other help to deal with the after-effects of a disaster.
  - Communicate with staff – over-communicate if necessary – about progress, moving back into the building, safety, etc. Make sure staff know whom to contact if there's a problem.
  - Make alternative arrangements for paying staff if routine mechanisms go out of action.

- alternative premises

  - Investigate a reciprocal arrangement for space with other organisations.

- continuity of operations and the level of service to be provided – the organisation needs to be operational as soon as possible, preferably the next day

  - Inform customers and suppliers and let them know where you can be contacted – customers will desert you if you are unavailable for weeks.
  - Brief the public relations spokesperson to deal with the media.

- physical communications

  - Investigate your telephone company's services – can they forward calls?
  - Plan for an ad hoc telephone directory and make sure your switchboard personnel know what to tell callers.
  - Decide where mail should be sent to.

- equipment and resources
  - Identify critical documents and their location so that vital material can be retrieved from the damaged building.
  - Store back-ups of material, including IT back-ups, off-site.
  - Work out what resources are needed during the recovery period and ensure these will be available.
  - Make sure cash is available at all times, but don't rush out and buy new equipment straight away – hiring may be a better option.
  - Investigate the possibility of establishing a resource network and identify cooperative partners with whom equipment, storage and costs could be shared.

Keep copies of the DP in a number of locations.

4. Test the plan with a pilot group

This will help to spot whether anything has been overlooked and give an indication of whether the plan would work in practice. How long does it take to set up the control centre? Will the communication systems work, even in the event of a natural disaster? Are the alternative premises suitable? Amend the plan as necessary to take into account any problems revealed by the pilot.

5. Communicate and implement the plan

A presentation should be made by a member of the disaster planning team to ensure all staff are aware of and understand the DP, its objectives and what to do in an emergency. Training will be an on-going process with new staff, and 'rehearsals' of emergency drills and reaction procedures should be carried out at least once a year to serve as a reminder for existing staff. Deal with any worries staff may have.

6. Monitor, revise and improve the plan

The DP is not set in stone – it should change with the circumstances. At intervals, at least annually, test out both individual components and the whole plan, and revise as necessary, taking into account impacts of new developments, such as new technology. Review reported disasters to see what can be learned to benefit your DP. Communicate any changes to staff.

Dos and don'ts for disaster planning

Do

- Be prepared.
- Learn from others' mistakes – and successes.
- Involve staff.
- Ensure all staff are aware of the plan.
- Communicate – with staff, customers, suppliers.
- Keep copies of the plan in a number of locations – it is no use if the plan itself is destroyed in the disaster!

Don't

- Be complacent – what if it did happen to you?
- Assume you've thought of everything – listen to comments and suggestions.
- Think of disaster planning as a one-off task – the plan must be kept up-to-date.

Useful reading

Books

Disaster planning for library and information services, John Ashman, London: Aslib, 1995

Continuity planning: preventing, surviving and recovering from disaster, Ronald D Ginn, Oxford: Elsevier Advanced Technology, 1989

Journal articles

Disaster management: controlling the plan, Graham Matthews, Managing Information, vol 1 no 7/8, Jul/Aug 1994, pp24–27

Bracing for emergencies, Charlene Marmer Solomon, Personnel Journal, vol 73 no 4, Apr 1994, pp74–76, 78, 80–83

The disaster business, Malcolm Brown, Management Today, Oct 1993, pp42–44, 47–48

Disaster and its aftermath, Lillian Gorman and Kathryn D McKee, HR Magazine, vol 35 no 3, Mar 1990, pp54–55, 57–58

Thought starters

- Have you ever been involved in a disaster? What can you learn from that experience?
- If a disaster did hit your organisation, would it survive?
- What risks does your organisation face and what can be done to minimise them?
- Can you afford not to have a disaster plan? The costs of a disaster are not just financial – they include interruption to business, wasted time and lost opportunities.

Health and Safety: Undertaking a Risk Assessment

This checklist provides a plan of action for those carrying out a risk assessment in their company or organisation.

The 1988 Control of Substances Hazardous to Health Regulations (COSHH) and the 1992 Associated Code of Practice for the Management of Health and Safety at Work Regulations require every organisation to undertake a risk assessment as part of their health and safety procedure. Failure to comply with the legislation can result in fines and/or imprisonment for senior managers or directors. By identifying hazards in the workplace and the likelihood of an accident occurring (the risk), employers can take action to deal with the most pressing problem areas. Reducing accidents in the workplace benefits both employer and employee through the creation of a safer working environment and savings due both to a reduction in lost time and productivity, and fewer accident claims. This checklist does not aim to cover the complex legal issues, for which expert advice should be sought.

MCI Standards

This checklist has relevance for the MCI Management Standards: Key Role A – Manage Activities.

Definition

A health and safety risk assessment is a planned procedure in which all hazards in the workplace are identified and the likelihood of an accident occurring through each of the hazards estimated.

Advantages

Risk assessments:

- comply with health and safety legislation
- make accident prevention easier by identifying hazards
- help to improve workforce morale by conveying a 'caring' attitude.

Disadvantages

There are no real disadvantages to carrying out a risk assessment, but remember that they:

- can require considerable resources (in staff time) to undertake thoroughly
- need to be updated each time a new piece of equipment or machinery is introduced.

Action checklist

1. Designate a Risk Assessment Committee

The members of the Risk Assessment Committee should be drawn from all levels of the organisation. The Committee will manage the implementation and running of the risk assessment. Appoint a coordinator (preferably, but not necessarily, from senior management – someone with project management experience who commands respect and can get things done) to oversee the project.

2. Define the scope and coverage of the assessment

Use the experience of the Committee if they have been involved in this type of scheme before. All types of risk must be assessed: however, it can be easier (depending on the size of the organisation) to identify and concentrate assessments on specific risks (for example manual handling) at any one time. Decide who is to be included in the assessment at this stage – all departments, or (for example) one site or one floor. Indicate who will carry out the assessment – a large organisation may need a number of individuals; in a small company one person may be sufficient. Remember that legislation states that the persons undertaking the assessment must be 'competent' – this term has not been defined in the Acts, but is taken to mean persons who have sufficient training and experience.

3. Design an assessment form

Create a form that the individual(s) involved in the assessment will use to record risks. Make wording simple and clear to understand. Include a rating scale for the severity of the risk, either in words (for example, very severe to slight risk) or numbers (for example 1=low risk and 5=high risk). Identify which employees are at risk and, if applicable, other individuals such as the general public. Leave space so that any suggestions for minimising the risk can be noted. Draw up a list of 'pointers' for the assessor to look for. In a general risk assessment these may include:

- fire – are there any flammable materials near sources of heat?
- manual handling – are employees carrying items that should be left to machines?
- chemicals – are all hazardous substances stored correctly?
- electricity – are any 'bare' wires visible?
- dust – are extractor fans removing all dust?
- temperature (high and low) – do room temperatures reach abnormal levels?
- noise – are there areas of excessive noise?
- tobacco smoke – are non-smokers at risk from 'passive smoking'?
- visual display units (VDUs) – are users straining their eyes to see the VDU?
- office equipment – do chairs and desks meet health and safety requirements?

The relevant legislation to check includes:

- 1988 and 1994 Control of Substances Hazardous to Health Act (COSHH)
- 1989 Noise at Work Regulations
- 1992 Management of Health and Safety at Work Regulations
- 1992 Health and Safety (Display Screen Equipment) Regulations
- 1992 Manual Handling Operations Regulations
- 1992 Personal Protective Equipment at Work Regulations
- 1992 Provision and Use of Work Equipment Regulations
- 1992 Workplace (Health, Safety and Welfare) Regulations
- 1997 Workplace (Fire Precautions) Regulations
- 1997 Health and Safety (Young Persons) Regulations.

If possible, use the accident book or 'near-miss' log for actual examples.

4. Train assessors in identifying risk

Identifying risks in the workplace is not an easy task. Where the individual who is to carry out the risk assessment is not a health and safety officer, it is essential to obtain appropriate training, either from an internal source if available, or from an external agency in order to be sure that they are 'competent'. The suppliers of equipment, machinery or chemicals can be a good source of advice.

It is important to train the assessors in rating the severity of a risk. Examples of hazards should be discussed with the trainee(s) to obtain some standardisation.

5. Communicate the assessment to employees

Let all employees know (using newsletters, notice boards, and team briefings) that a risk assessment is to be undertaken and who the assessor(s) will be. Invite them to look out for any hazards that should be included in the assessment and if they find one ask them to inform their supervisor or the person responsible for the assessment in their area.

6. Draw up a plan for the assessments

Plan a timetable of when the various areas will be assessed and at what point the assessment will be complete. Build into the timetable a schedule noting availability of Risk Assessment Committee members to ensure that at least one is on hand to assist with procedural difficulties.

7. Carry out the assessment

8. Record the results

The Risk Assessment Committee must collate all of the completed assessment forms and analyse the results. Look for problem areas, such as one department with a large number of high risks. Create a list of all the risks in order of severity and report them to senior management. Keep this documentation for external health and safety officials, and as an internal record to check for changes made.

Look for any difficulties individuals had in completing the assessment; extra training may be needed for future assessments, or the assessment form may require modifications.

9. Report back to employees

A requirement of the health and safety legislation is that feedback must be given to employees of the results of the assessment. Notify them of any proposed changes to reduce the risk of accidents.

10. Take action

Consider what action should be taken to eliminate or minimize the risks identified and draw up a plan for implementing the necessary changes.

Dos and don'ts of undertaking a risk assessment

Do

- Involve workers on the 'shop floor'.
- Check the accident or 'near-miss' log.
- Ensure assessors are adequately trained.
- Seek advice from suppliers of any new equipment, machinery or chemicals.

Don't

- Think of it as a one-off assessment – action must be taken on the results and reviewed and updated.
- Ignore any risk as being too small.
- Forget to keep written documentation of the assessment.

Useful reading

BOOKS

The complete guide to business risk management, Kit Sadgrove, Aldershot: Gower, 1996
Health risk management: practical guidance for managers in small and medium sized enterprises, Sudbury: HSE Books, 1995
Risk assessment: a line managers guide, Pat McGuiness, London: Industrial Society, 1995

JOURNAL ARTICLES

Assess your business safety, Small Business Confidential, no 166, June 1997, pp2–3
Health and safety risk assessment, Lawrence Waterman and Rob Lane, Company Secretary's Review, Vol 20 no 5, 16 April 1997, pp193–194
Raising a risk profile, Paul Hopkin, Health and Safety at Work, Vol 18 no 1, January 1996, pp16–18

Useful addresses

Health and Safety Executive, Rose Court, 2 Southwark Bridge, London, SE1 9HS, Tel: 0171 717 6000
Royal Society for the Prevention of Accidents, Edgbaston Park, 353 Bristol Road, Birmingham, B5 7ST, Tel: 0121 248 2000

Thought starters

- Have you ever been involved in an accident at work?
- Can you think of anything potentially dangerous in your workplace?
- How could you make your workplace safer?
- Has poor equipment ever caused damage/harm to personnel?

Health and Safety: Managing the Process

This checklist provides an overview of the key issues that should be considered in managing the health and safety process within an organisation. Effective health and safety management is not just a legal and moral obligation, but a personal one, as managers are increasingly being held personally accountable in law for the safety of their employees.

To succeed, top management commitment is required to support a coherent strategy that is fully integrated into the general management practice of the organisation.

Definition

Management of the health and safety process involves the setting of a policy, creation of a suitable organisational culture, development and implementation of a health and safety plan, and evaluation of the plan's performance.

Advantages of managing the health and safety process

Managing health and safety effectively not only ensures that you meet legislative requirements but also:

- contributes to the positive well-being of the organisation
- reduces the risk of injury and ill health
- reduces lost staff time
- improves corporate image and averts negative publicity
- contributes towards a programme of continuous improvement.

Disadvantages of managing the health and safety process

The benefits far outweigh the disadvantages, but managing health and safety properly:

- takes up time and resources
- requires constant review and updating.

Action checklist

1. Get the policy right

Success relies on an effective policy which minimises health and safety risks to employees and others. Key actions at this stage include:

- undertaking a health and safety risk assessment – this will give you information on areas that need attention and monitoring
- familiarising yourself with relevant legislation (see Useful Reading)
- allocating responsibilities for creating and revising health and safety policy and procedures
- ensuring that the health and safety policy is given the same priority as your other organisational goals
- resourcing health and safety adequately – using a separate budget if appropriate.

2. Create a positive health and safety culture

The creation of a culture which secures the motivation and involvement of all members of the organisation in health and safety is critical. All employees need to think 'safety first' and consider health and safety matters as a natural part of their working life.

You can create the right climate for this to develop in some of the following ways:

- appoint health and safety champions to raise the profile and drive the project
- set health and safety objectives and performance standards for all staff – remember that prevention is better than cure
- involve employees and safety representatives at all stages – from planning through implementation to monitoring and review
- provide adequate information on health and safety to all staff and keep them up to date
- implement refresher training for all staff at regular intervals
- reward employees for good health and safety practice
- include health and safety as an agenda item at management meetings and team briefings.

3. Develop a plan

You will need to:

- produce a written plan for health and safety which is reviewed regularly – co-ordinate and timetable all health and safety activities in one programme
- identify clear objectives and standards

- include measurable targets
- identify resources required
- consider all the processes in your organisation – from purchasing materials to delivering the product or service – and all personnel when drawing up a plan.

Areas which the plan may look at include:

- **accident prevention** – look at severe hazards such as chemicals and radiation, and also more common hazards such as trailing electrical leads and heavy lifting
- **physical working conditions** – including factors such as light, heat, ventilation, seating, hygiene and computer workstations
- **psychological health** – covering areas such as stress reduction, shift working, rest breaks, prevention of bullying and achieving a work-family balance
- **health problems of employees** – including alcoholism and drug addiction
- **health promotion** – for example exercise and healthy eating
- **emergency procedures** – such as fire drills, equipment shutdown and security procedures
- **specific groups of employees particularly at risk** – including the young, disabled workers and pregnant women.

Depending on the nature of your business, you may also need to consider extending your health and safety plan to suppliers and contractors. Any failings on their part will impact on your organisation, so a written policy and penalties for non-compliance could be introduced.

Remember also to consider the health and safety of customers using your products or services and of visitors to your premises.

4. Measure performance

Once your plan is in place, you will need to ensure it is effective. Performance can be measured proactively as well as reactively. Proactive measures include:

- auditing your system to ensure that monitoring systems are in place and are effective
- systematically inspecting the workplace
- evaluating your training processes
- talking to staff
- reviewing the relevant minutes of management meetings.

Reactive measures include:

- examining data collected after incidents – accident books, sickness records and records of 'near misses'
- checking damage to property, perhaps via insurance reporting.

Performance evaluation will enable you to check that your policy and plans are working efficiently and continue to meet objectives and changing circumstances. The evaluation process might involve:

- comparing your findings to your objectives and standards
- validating your findings by talking to staff
- benchmarking against similar organisations in your area
- giving feedback to staff and seeking commitment to improvements
- changing your policy, plan and procedures to reflect your findings – ensure that high risk areas are given priority attention.

Review will be a continuous process, but you will need to set a timetable for formally revising your health and safety plan every year, or when new legislation or regulations require it.

Dos and don'ts for managing the health and safety process

Do
- Involve all your staff.
- Give health and safety the same priority as your organisational goals.
- Aim for continuous improvement.
- Consider health and safety issues when carrying out organisation restructuring – if necessary, arrange training for those taking on new health and safety responsibilities.

Don't
- Assume that health and safety is only for high-risk or hazardous environments.
- Assume that health and safety is just 'common sense' and therefore understood by everyone.
- Forget to include temporary staff and contractors in your planning.

Useful reading
Workplace health, safety and welfare, Health and Safety Executive, Sudbury: HSE Books, 1997

Consulting employees on health and safety: a guide to the law, Health and Safety Executive, 1996

Managing people: health and safety, Institute of Management Foundation, London: Pitman, 1995

Essentials of health and safety at work, 3rd ed, Health and Safety Executive, Sudbury: HSE Books, 1995

Health and safety for busy managers: law, risks and liabilities, Ann T Holder, Hitchin: Technical Communications, 1995

Successful health and safety management, Health and Safety Executive, London: HMSO, 1991

Useful addresses

Health and Safety Executive, Rose Court, 2 Southwark Bridge, London, SE1 9HS, Tel: 0171 717 6000

Royal Society for the Prevention of Accidents, Cannon House, Prior Queensway, Birmingham, B4 6BS, Tel: 0121 200 2461

British Safety Council, 70 Chancellor's Road, London, W6 9RS, Tel: 0181 741 1231

Thought starters

- How much money are you losing by not managing health and safety effectively?
- Talk to your staff – how aware are they of health and safety risks and issues in your workplace?
- Who is responsible for health and safety in your organisation? How accountable are they?
- Are there any incentives in place to encourage good health and safety practice?

Note: This checklist was prepared in collaboration with the Health and Safety Executive's Operations Unit.

Internal Audit

This checklist is designed to help managers tackle the process of an internal audit within their organisation or department. Internal audit is an essential part of business life, but not all organisations are large enough to have a designated internal audit function. This checklist is aimed primarily at those who are either undertaking an internal audit themselves or are responsible for selecting and managing a member of staff who has this responsibility. It applies equally to organisations in the public and private sectors.

MCI Standards

This checklist has relevance for the MCI Management Standards: Key Roles A, B and F – Manage Activities, Manage Resources and Manage Quality.

Definition

There is a clear distinction between internal and external audit. Internal auditing is defined by the Institute of Internal Auditors as an independent appraisal function established within an organisation to examine and evaluate its activities, the objective being to assist staff in the effective discharge of their responsibilities. To this end internal auditing furnishes staff with analyses, appraisals and recommendations concerning those activities. Internal auditing is usually carried out by staff from within the organisation.

Advantages of internal audit

Internal audit should be a continuous process, from which many advantages can be discerned. These may include:

- management's attention will be directed to the key business issues – it gives an analysis of weaknesses in the system of control, from which practical recommendations for improvement can be made
- it leads to positive assurance when controls are operating satisfactorily
- it identifies opportunities for improved efficiency and effectiveness
- it gives early notice of potential problems. Management can then take action as necessary.

Disadvantages of internal audit

- It can be time-consuming and takes managers away from their day-to-day work.
- If handled insensitively, it can be threatening to staff who may feel that they are being scrutinised with the intention of finding fault.

Action checklist

1. Select internal audit objectives relevant to the assignment

Internal audits primarily look at key controls:

- financial – how is money handled within the organisation? Questions like who authorises payment, and what are the checks and balances to stop unauthorised spending and fraud?
- administrative controls – are these conducive to meeting strategic objectives?
- systems – which ones are there in a department and across the organisation – and how do they fit together?

as well as:

- value for money – is this being achieved through the systems in place, or do the systems fail to measure this?

The first step is to make sure your broad audit objectives reflect whichever of these are your priorities.

2. Prepare a detailed brief

An internal audit looks at a variety of aspects of the way an organisation works. It does not only focus on financial issues. Write an audit brief or strategy to set detailed priorities in accordance with the main issues, and give some indication of the proportion of time you expect to be accorded to highlighted aspects.

3. Choose your auditor

It is usual to appoint another individual from within the organisation as internal auditor. Dependent on the issues to be examined, a formal qualification, for example, in accountancy, may be appropriate.

The growing use of external certification systems for issues such as quality control (ISO9000), environmental control (ISO14000) and staff development (Investors In People) may require other members of staff to have responsibility for the continuous review of those systems.

4. Brief your auditor

You need to make sure that you have all the background information you need before you brief your auditor. This would include your organisation's:

- strategic or business plans
- standing orders
- articles and memoranda of association
- internal procedure manuals
- lists of key personnel
- structure chart.

Arrange a meeting to ensure you have provided the auditor with sufficient information; in particular, even if he or she is an employee of the organisation do not make assumptions about his or her level of knowledge.

At the meeting the aim is to agree the objectives of the audit. Find out how the auditor will meet these objectives, agree a timetable and a plan of action and find out if further information is needed.

5. Identify the key controls to meet audit objectives

The next stage is to start to look at detail. The auditor needs to look at the organisation's existing procedures for controlling the key areas to be examined.

6. Evaluate the controls

Next, evaluate how effective the controls are. Could they be improved? Are there any omissions? Questions worth thinking about are:

- if someone wanted to commit a fraud, where and how would they do it?
- if I had bought this item personally, would I be happy with the price paid and the level of service offered?

7. Test the system

Now, test the controls in action. Choose a number of activities or transactions at random and trace back all the steps that took place. Ask:

- are there any procedures or rules in place?
- did people follow the procedures?

This will show how far the existing rules and procedures are complied with.

8. Select areas needing in-depth investigation

From random tests the auditor may find areas of concern which need further investigation. The audit should now investigate these areas in depth – for example every transaction will be examined over a number of months to see if the random sample was an exception or a real problem.

9. Consider whether value for money is being achieved

Whatever the overall audit objectives, it is always an internal auditor's job to test whether value for money is being achieved. The kind of things to look for are:

- has the market been tested by getting quotes and tenders for goods and services?
- are the systems working in the most efficient way?

10. Prepare a draft report

Make a report of all findings with a set of recommendations. This should be in draft format and should be discussed with everyone who took part in the audit – to ensure that the auditor hasn't misinterpreted any information.

11. Produce the final report

The final report should include an action plan to tackle the areas requiring strengthening. It should have a timetable and an agreed time to meet again to monitor what has happened. Use the knowledge of the auditor as a guide towards best practice. Make sure the recommendations in the report are of a practical nature.

12. Take action

Act on the findings to put things right and monitor how effective the actions taken are. This may well involve changing written instructions, manuals or procedures, alerting staff to the changes and ensuring adequate training is given to staff in those areas.

Dos and don'ts for internal audits

Do

- Brief staff on the benefits of internal audit.
- Keep staff informed of the findings of the audit and any positive action that has been taken as a result of it.
- Concentrate on the high risk elements identified.
- Set an action plan that is realistic.
- Monitor progress towards meeting the action plan.

Don't

- Rely on internal audit as a day-to-day management control mechanism.
- Expect internal audit to pick up all the potential weak links in your systems.

Useful reading

BOOKS

Standards and guidelines for the professional practice of internal auditing, London: Institute of Internal Auditors, 1998

Self assessment: a tool for integrated management, Keith Beasley, Cheltenham: Stanley Thornes, 1994

Managing the internal audit: a practical handbook, Ian Beale and Roy H Bradford, London: Kogan Page, 1993

JOURNAL ARTICLES

Understanding internal audit, Peter Rickard, Australian Accountant, Vol 64 no 3, Apr 1994, pp30–32, 34

Audit reports in the 1990s, Peter Rickard, Australian Accountant, Vol 63 no 1, Feb 1993, pp19–23

Useful addresses

Institute of Internal Auditors, 13 Abbeville Mews, 88 Clapham Park Road, London, SW4 7BX, Tel: 0171 498 0101

Thought starters

- Have you defined the nature and scope of the internal audit?
- Have you established what the system is trying to achieve?
- Have you identified the key controls?
- Are your staff fully informed of what is happening and the actions you are going to take?

Mapping Human Resource Skills

This checklist is for those organisations that wish to obtain detailed information on the skills of their employees. Although skills mapping exists in many organisations on an informal networking basis, few organisations have a formal programme for tapping into the largely unused skills of their employees.

MCI Standards

This checklist has relevance for the MCI Management Standards: Key Roles C and D – Manage People and Manage Information.

Definition

A skill is the ability to perform a task proficiently. In the context of this checklist, skills are not restricted to those necessary (or useful) to carry out the task someone was employed to do. A mapping scheme aims to track skills that aren't currently being utilised but could be needed in the future, or can be used in the organisation now though not part of the employee's job description.

Advantages of mapping human resource skills

Mapping human resource skills:

- saves money by using identified in-house skills
- helps in planning for the future
- helps utilise your employees' skills better
- identifies areas of strength and weakness within the organisation
- helps in the recruitment process as skills gaps can be identified
- enhances the feel-good factor as organisations become interested in the 'whole' being
- motivates employees, especially those at lower levels who take pride in using a particular skill for the benefit of the organisation.

Disadvantages of mapping human resource skills

The process:

- needs constant updating to remain accurate and useful
- requires a fairly substantial commitment of staff time (certainly at the beginning of the project)
- may lead to staff being required to use skills they possess but don't wish to use.

Action checklist

1. Obtain management backing

As the time and resources needed to collect the skills of employees are considerable, it is essential that the project has the commitment of senior management.

Appoint a coordinator, someone with project management experience, who commands respect and can get things done, to oversee the project. Estimate the cost of collecting and analysing the data.

2. Define the terms of reference

Identify the employees to be covered by the system (for example, will it exclude shopfloor workers?). Try to define what types of skill should be recorded (for example, formal qualifications or knowledge of a foreign language). Include areas of experience that an employee has, for example, the setting up and installation of a computer system or a just-in-time scheme.

3. Assign responsibility

One person should be given responsibility for the collection of the skills data from each section or department in the organisation. They will be the ones who will have to keep the skills system up-to-date in their area.

Consult with the IT department about obtaining a suitable piece of software to hold the skills data or whether existing software can be modified. It may be possible to link or share data with personnel records if they are already computerised. Ask for their assistance in training those inputting the skills data on to the system.

4. Formulate a data collection method

Three methods are available for collecting the skills data:

- Questionnaire – for each employee to complete and return. Questionnaires are difficult to design and can be filled in badly, but they are a relatively inexpensive way of collecting the skills data.

- Interview – by an assigned person and the employee. More time-consuming than using questionnaires but can be useful in drawing out more information from employees.
- Combination of questionnaire and interview – where the employee completes an initial questionnaire followed up by an interview as necessary.

The combination is the preferred method, but the resources available to the project will be the crucial factor in deciding which collection method is used. Whether questionnaires or interviews are used, or both, they need to be carefully structured, for example, to prompt respondents who may not think of a particular aptitude as a skill.

5. Train staff in data collection

The staff who have been assigned to collect the skills data should be trained thoroughly in what types of skills to include and how they should be input on to the computer system. Practice interviews are a useful way of doing this. Guidelines should be drawn up and distributed.

6. Pay close attention to the Data Protection Act

If your organisation is registered under the Data Protection Act, the skills database concept may already be covered. Check with the nominated contact within your organisation.

If you are not already registered or are not covered by the existing registration, you must contact the Data Protection Registrar, who will keep a record of the:

- personal data held by the data user
- purposes for which the data is used
- sources from which the data was obtained
- people to whom the data may be disclosed
- overseas countries to which the personal data may be transferred.

Registered data users must comply with the data protection principles which state that personal information shall be:

- collected fairly and lawfully
- used only for the purposes stated in the register
- adequate, relevant and not excessive to the purposes stated
- accurate, up-to-date and not held for longer than necessary
- accessible to the individual concerned, who, where appropriate, has the right to have information about him / herself corrected or erased
- kept secure.

An individual can seek compensation through the courts if damage is caused by the loss, destruction, inaccuracy or unauthorised disclosure of personal data held by a data user, so pay special attention to this area.

7. Communicate the system to all employees

It is very important that the scheme is promoted to all employees whose skills will be registered. Advantages to be gained by the employees should be communicated and fears about 'Big Brother' dealt with. Possible benefits of the scheme can be given as:

- greater utilisation of an employee's skills, leading to greater job satisfaction
- more varied work, as employees from different departments may be brought together to form cross-functional teams
- an increase in internal promotion as suitable in-house candidates can be searched for easily.

Successful promotion of the scheme will not only help in getting employees to take part but should also make them more likely to actively volunteer information when they acquire a new skill.

8. Draw up a timetable

Depending on the size of the organisation, it can be useful to pilot the collection of the skills data on one site or in one large department. This will give you some idea of any problem areas requiring modifications to the system. The timetable will indicate deadlines for each section's skills data to be passed on to the coordinator. Set a target date for the scheme to be completed and fully operational.

9. Implement the scheme

Inform the employees of the person who will be collecting the data in their department or on their site, how the data will be collected, and of a contact who is available to answer any questions regarding the scheme.

Collect and input the data. Promote the system within the organisation and make sure it is used, for example to fill a new post in-house or to put together a project team.

10. Evaluate the success of the system

Opinions should be sought from users of the scheme and employees as to its usefulness. Communicate successes to employees, for example an internal promotion or the completion of a project which had used the system to create a team containing the necessary skills. Make sure you don't forget to collect any complaints or grievances about the scheme and make any necessary changes.

11. Keep the system up-to-date

An out-of-date list of skills may do more harm than good. Remember to update the system at regular periods, at least once a year. Always remove individuals' details when they leave and add new employees to the system when they start.

Dos and don'ts for mapping human resource skills

Do

- Update the skills database regularly.
- Make employees aware of the benefits of the database to them.
- Communicate successful uses of the database.

Don't

- Think that any skill is irrelevant just because there is no immediate need for it (for example fluent French).
- Forget about the security of the information held on the database.

Useful reading

BOOK

The handbook of human resource planning, Gordon McBeath, Oxford: Blackwell, 1992

JOURNAL ARTICLES

Setting up an electronic job posting system, Sharon M Tarrant, Training and Development USA, Vol 48 no 1, January 1994, pp39–42

Management analysis and planning for skill development in the 90s, Roscoe H Adams, SAM Advanced Management Journal, Vol 54 no 4, Autumn 1989, pp34–40

A computer based employee skills inventory system, Robert V Lorenzo, Journal of Managerial Psychology, Vol 3 no 2, 1988, pp5–9

Skills bank tracks talent not training, Amiel T Sharon, Personnel Journal, Vol 67 no 6, June 1988, pp44–49

How high tech helped uncover hidden talents, Garry Winsor, Personnel Management, Vol 20 no 3, March 1988, pp48–51

Useful address

The Data Protection Registrar, Wycliffe House, Water Lane, Wilmslow, Cheshire SK9 5AF, Tel: 01625 545745

Thought starters

- Do you know what skills your staff have?
- Do you have any skill / knowledge that is not currently being used?
- Have you struggled to complete a task because the appropriate skills were not available to you?
- Have you ever discovered after a project was completed that a fellow employee had just the skill you were looking for?
- Have you gone 'outside' for a skill and later learned it was available in-house?

Using the Internet for Business

> This checklist provides an outline of the issues associated with using the Internet for business.

MCI Standards

This checklist has relevance for the MCI Management Standards: Key Roles B and D – Manage Resources and Manage Information.

Definition

The Internet is a worldwide network of computer networks, connected to each other by telecommunications links via one of the national backbone networks (such as SuperJanet in the UK). Initially the Internet was used primarily by the military, academics and computer enthusiasts who developed their own code of ethics: that of mutual help and exchange of information. Increasingly commercial organisations are making use of the Internet. The typical Internet user is no longer an 'anorak', nor yet predominantly a 'suit'. Although business use is increasing rapidly, in reality, a wide cross-section of the population is now connected as numbers of users in the UK top 7 million, in the USA 50 million, and worldwide, 100 million.

Benefits of using the Internet

The Internet:

- enables cheap and efficient long-distance communication
- offers unlimited potential for personal networking
- has worldwide marketing potential
- opens up worldwide sources of information
- offers as much security and confidentiality as other communications media
- offers a worldwide common platform for business transactions.

Drawbacks of using the Internet

It:

- still largely only carries information which organisations give away free of charge
- includes information which can be incomplete, illegal, trivial or of questionable quality
- uses only recently developed secure payment systems which are still not yet widely trusted by sellers or buyers
- can be slow, both to connect with and to use
- can be time-consuming and threaten users with information overload.

Action checklist

1. Why bother with the Internet?

Largely because the spirit of the Internet is in tune with current changes in the marketplace and ways of exploring new ways of work. The Internet provides a platform for innovation and creativity, for exploring flexible ways of working, for creating new relationships with new suppliers and customers, and – without getting too carried away – for reaching markets beyond traditional scope.

The Internet is also evolving very rapidly. There is no real evidence for saying that those who leave it late to get on to the Internet will suffer, but latecomers will have a lot of learning, trial, error and experience to catch up with.

2. Familiarise yourself with what the Internet can do

Electronic mail (e-mail) offers a much cheaper and highly effective alternative to sending and receiving messages.

The World Wide Web (WWW) is a medium for disseminating information on a world-wide scale and a forum which is developing for buying and selling. The WWW is a program which cross-references, links and retrieves data from computers around the world, using hypertext which allows you to move from document to document using a mouse to click on highlighted terms or graphics.

Newsgroups and Discussion Lists enable the exchange of ideas with colleagues, known and unknown, all over the world who share the same interests.

File transfer protocol (FTP) allows you to transfer a file held on one computer to another as an alternative to sending it on disk or paper through the post.

3. Explore the relevance of the Internet to your business

Examine the potential of the Internet for reducing costs and increasing the scope and effectiveness of your business in the following areas:

Information gathering and market research: information quality is improving as commercial publishers establish their platforms on the Web. This may be at a price, but will provide the reliability and consistency lacking in the first days of the Web.

Communication and information dissemination: e-mail enables extremely low-cost messaging across borders and time zones to customers, suppliers and partners alike.

Marketing and commercial transactions: as problems of security and confidentiality are overcome, it is likely that an increasing number of commercial transactions will be made on the World Wide Web.

Delivery of services: as well as the possibility of straightforward selling on the Internet, there is also the possibility of delivering added-value services. These may be existing services offered in a new format, such as electronic newspapers or distance-based training courses, or new services specifically created to take advantage of the new medium – at the moment these tend to be consultancy-oriented, such as Web site design, but they are growing and diversifying.

4. Examine the business issues

This means becoming aware of:

The growing area of **Internet law** – especially in the area of intellectual property and copyright. There have already been test cases over the ownership – and therefore rights – of material on Web sites.

Issues of **Security** – such as protecting your information from corruption or the dangers of degradation through hackers and viruses by using firewalls and anti-virus software

Information overload – seeking measures and procedures which can eliminate the threat of being swamped by the mass of information available through the Newsgroups and the Web

Issues of **control** – examining the dangers – as well as the potential gain – of providing organisation-wide access to all the services available on the Internet, and deciding who should have access to what.

The possibilities of **buying and selling on the Web** – the WWW is moving beyond its former limits as a marketing device to one where business and financial transactions are becoming the norm. Many major banks and software houses are collaborating on secure financial transactions using various forms of encryption, ensuring that confidential data between buyer and seller travels in safety.

It is predicted to be only a short period of time before exploration of commercial transactions is converted into widespread usage, as confidence spreads.

5. Decide which form of access you require

Large organisations have set up permanent connections to the Internet. This means that their employees enjoy a faster capability for sending and receiving information. Other users access the Internet via a dial-up connection from their PC to a commercial Internet Access Provider. Here the connection is not open all the time but is only activated when the user dials up the Internet Access Provider. This means that e-mail can be sent and received only when the link is open.

Costs of access will vary according to the needs of the subscriber. At the bottom end of the market, an Internet Access Provider will charge around £150 a year for a single simple dial-up connection suitable for the purpose of evaluating the Internet. At the other extreme, full connectivity with very fast connections can run into tens of thousands of pounds; the cost includes a dedicated, leased telecommunications line and maintaining a server for Internet traffic.

6. Develop a strategic approach to Internet operations

A Web site can be fun to design and pack lots of promise into the beginning of an electronic future. However:

- Decide early on how you are going to measure success:

  - by numbers of visitors?
  - by numbers of business enquiries which can be followed up?
  - by cost-savings elsewhere?
  - by direct increase in overall sales?

- Decide who is out there as a potential customer. There are now over 100 million people on the Internet. Categories of users are now being identified through research.

- Decide whether your products or services are suitable for marketing through the Internet. Early research suggests that even traditional manufacturing companies can benefit from taking creative and interactive approaches, such as inviting visitors to design their own car and then test drive it! The major market for development, however, would appear to be in the domain of information services and publications which can be sold on – and through – the Internet.

- Decide what information you want on your Web site and who is to control and update it.

- Decide who in the organisation is to have access. This will largely depend on the culture of the organisation and what kind of grey area exists between trust and supervision. If access is available to all, assess how this might change the information power-base of the organisation. The Internet is a final step in shifting information from a privilege to a working tool which can be acted on – and reacted to – in no time at all.

7. Is the Internet for you?

It is difficult to merely tinker with the Internet. The world is already divided into those who can't live without it and those who can. If the organisation is going to exploit the Internet, it will cost more in terms of exploration and research than first imagined – time and effort are easily absorbed in ever greater quantities. But the Internet will also change the way you work – over time. In the beginning reflect on the:

- liberalisation of information flow which the Internet engenders
- possibilities for flexible working
- skill levels required of staff responsible for Internet operations and training for those who will be using it.

Think of the Internet as a cost-centre of the present and an investment for the future. If commercial gain is a target, then the Internet is unlikely to recoup its costs in the short-term.

Dos and don'ts associated with using the Internet

Do
- Safeguard your computer (especially if it is on a network and if you have a permanent connection to the Internet) against hackers and viruses.
- Ensure that your organisation's use of the Internet is appropriate to its short and long term objectives.
- Assign the responsibility of the project to somebody who is knowledgeable or is enthusiastic to learn.

Don't
- Forget to monitor all the cost implications.
- Become swayed by the hyperbole.

Useful reading

Teach yourself the Internet in business, Bob Norton and Cathy Smith, London: Hodder & Stoughton, 1998

Understanding business on the Internet in a week, Bob Norton and Cathy Smith, London: Hodder & Stoughton, 1996

Successful selling on the Internet in a week, Carol O Connor, London: Hodder & Stoughton, 1997

The Internet strategy handbook: lessons from the new frontier of business, Mary J Cronin, Boston, Mass: Harvard Business School Press, 1996

Thought starters

- Has one of your suppliers or customers got an e-mail address?
- Do any of your competitors have a presence on the Internet?

Preparing for Business Abroad

This checklist aims to stimulate thoughts about some of the implications of doing business abroad – of doing business with people of other nationalities, races and cultures. Success in doing business abroad often depends on 'getting the little things right' – recognising and anticipating cultural differences. The purpose of this checklist is to help you do that by pointing out some general guidelines and some specific examples. It is not a manual on foreign trade.

MCI Standards

This checklist has relevance for the MCI Management Standards: Key Role A – Manage Activities.

Definition

For the purposes of this checklist 'doing business abroad' involves either transacting business with people from other countries or transacting business in a country outside Britain. In doing business abroad you will be confronted with people of nationalities, races and cultures other than your own, and probably with customs, practices and legal systems which differ from yours.

Advantages of preparing for business abroad

It:

- increases your self-confidence in a situation which might be stressful
- enables you to appear informed and international in your outlook
- reduces the chances of your being taken by surprise by suddenly discovering that 'they' do things differently
- reduces the chances of you and your colleagues on the one hand, and of your potential business partners on the other, being embarrassed
- reduces the possibility of misunderstanding and increases the possibility of mutual understanding.

Action checklist

1. Identify sources of information

Write to, ring or even visit the embassy in Britain of the country you are visiting. Most have some literature about their countries which will provide useful background. In the case of some smaller countries, particularly those less economically developed, don't count on printed information being completely up-to-date.

Don't expect all embassy buildings to be like those of the United States or other major powers in the world. Some embassies consist of no more than two or three rooms on an upper floor. If you intend to visit an embassy, make a telephone call first to discover the hours during which it will be open to visitors. They are not all open 9.00am–5.00pm daily! In some embassies the staff will speak perfect English but in others they may not – be prepared for this if you speak to embassy staff on the telephone.

Once you are in the country which you are visiting, remember the British Embassy and, if it has an office in the country, the British Council, as sources of information.

Other sources of information include the Department of Trade and Industry, newspaper databases and the Financial Times' country profiles. And don't despise books intended for the tourist – they may contain useful information that is not available elsewhere (for example on tipping or good places to eat). The best source may be someone who has recently been to the country.

2. Decide what you need to know

- Find out the principal and minority languages of the country you are visiting. Mistaken assumptions can be embarrassing. Most countries in South America speak Spanish (with some differences which should not cause problems if you know Spanish) but Brazilians do not.

- Find out something about the history of the country you are visiting, especially its more recent history. In the case of the countries of Eastern Europe, recent histories may be complex but it is as well to know the influences which other countries may have had on the country in question.

- Discover whether there are significant minorities in the country. There are for example 600,000 ethnic Hungarians in Slovakia out of a population of 5 million. Their presence can have a major impact on the relationships between neighbours. Don't forget you may be attempting to do business with a member of a minority or mixed group.

- Discover something about your host country's internal politics but refrain from comment on them. It is impossible to know the alignment of your hosts and again in Eastern Europe and the states of the former USSR you must be careful. Many have adopted new political labels without changing their views, ambitions or allegiances.

- Discover something also about a country's religion. Many countries have more than one major religion although religious activity may be limited. Don't assume that all countries observe the same religious festivals as Britain or that they observe them in the same way or even on the same dates – many countries have a lot more public holidays than Britain, and you need to know when they are if you are not to find that some of your time in that country is wasted. Sundays are not always a 'day of rest' (cf Israel).

- Find out what temperatures and humidity are likely to be during your visit, so you can take suitable clothing.

3. Establish whether you need a visa

You may or may not need a visa – an authorisation, fixed or stamped in your passport, by your intended host country – in order to visit it. A travel agent can advise you on this, but it is often sensible to approach the embassy of your intended host. The embassy will issue a visa if you require one. Don't assume that you can obtain a visa instantly. You may need to fill in a very complex form; you may need to produce passport-size photographs; you will need to produce a valid passport. You may have to wait for several days; you may or may not have to pay for the visa. It is usually much quicker to go to the embassy in person than to do the transaction by mail.

4. Sort out foreign currency

Seek the advice of your bank or travel agent on what you should take. It may be possible to take some of your host country's currency but this is not always the case. Deutschmarks or US Dollars may be acceptable in the country you are visiting and travellers' cheques are a good stand-by.

It is probably advisable if you intend to take US Dollars only to take those issued during the last five years. Older ones are not acceptable in some countries where counterfeit dollars have been circulated in large numbers. Order currency in advance.

Unless you are a very experienced traveller, prepare a matrix giving at least approximate exchange cross rates of:

- the pound
- the local currency (know its subdivision)
- the US Dollar
- the Euro
- the Deutschmark
- the Japanese Yen.

Find out in advance whether, or which, credit cards you may use abroad; whether they are accepted in shops and restaurants; whether they can be used to obtain local currency at banks; whether they can be used in cash dispensers and:

- be prepared to pay a bank commission if you use your credit card to obtain currency
- be prepared to produce your passport at the same time if you want to avoid a journey back to your hotel
- don't obtain too much cash at once – find out in advance what your bank in Britain will accept if you bring foreign currency back (certainly not coins and possibly not notes from certain countries). Some countries do not permit you to take their currency out. Also, in countries with rapid inflation you can lose money by changing too much at once.

5. Find out about the local culture

As a starting point, check out the following aspects of culture:

- Tips – local custom may or may not require them. The amount and way of giving a tip (especially in a restaurant) may not follow our practice. Some require tips for taxis and not for restaurants, others vice-versa. Don't assume a standard rate of tipping applies across all services. In some countries expectations differ according to the area or city you are in (New York cab drivers expect 15%, in Chicago 10% will do.)
- Find out the locally acceptable practice for giving and receiving gifts.
- Don't be surprised by local toilet arrangements – mixed toilets supervised by a woman are not unknown. It is better to be prepared than shocked.
- Find out what is and what is not good manners. The belch which must be avoided at home may be obligatory in some countries to show appreciation of your host's cuisine. Some countries have unusual customs. In Norway, for example, if you are invited to a person's home for a meal, you are expected to make a speech afterwards praising the dinner and the hostess. People are sometimes very critical of their country – but can be offended if you agree with them.
- Find out about travel arrangements before you take a taxi or board a tram. It may be at least desirable to negotiate a taxi fare in advance. It may be necessary to purchase a tram ticket from a newsagent – and to cancel the ticket yourself on the tram. Find out about tickets first – and then watch the other passengers.
- Know something about the local police. Do they issue on-the-spot fines? For what?
- Be cautious about the local sense of humour. Few of us could describe our national or personal sense of humour. Some laugh at themselves; some only at their neighbours. Some who laugh at themselves don't like others to laugh at them.

- Learn about physical gestures – a nod in Bulgaria signifies lack of agreement.
- Don't make jokes about former communists or socialist institutions in Eastern Europe. You may be talking to a former communist about an institution which he managed. Only your order book may reflect his reaction.
- Accept hospitality carefully – 'pace it'. Your hosts may be used to whatever exotic drink you are taking – you may not.

Dos and don'ts in preparing for business abroad

Do

- Remember that people from other countries and cultures are as proud of their histories, cultures and achievements as you are.
- Remember the importance of listening.
- Know a few words in the language of your potential business partners – salutations especially.
- Try to know what is likely to be in the news headlines of the country during the period of your discussions and perhaps something of the background to those news items.
- Avoid religious issues.

Don't

- Patronise your contacts.
- Criticise the country's politicians – they may support them.
- Criticise the sanitary arrangements or standards of hygiene: just be grateful that you don't have to live with them.
- Make assumptions based on your standards, customs and practices.

Useful reading

Management worldwide, David J Hickson and Derek S Pugh, London: Penguin Books, 1995

Bargaining across borders: how to negotiate business successfully anywhere in the world, Dean Allen Foster, New York: McGraw Hill, 1995

Debrett's guide to business etiquette: the complete book of modern business practice and etiquette, Nicholas Yapp, London: Headline, 1994

Dos and taboos around the world, 3rd ed, Roger E Axtell, New York: John Wiley, 1993

We Europeans, 4th ed, Richard Hill, Brussels: Europublications, 1993

The dos and taboos of international trade: a small business primer, Roger E Axtell, New York: John Wiley, 1989

Thought starters

- What treatment by a foreigner would embarrass or annoy you?
- What stereotypes come into your mind when you think of the foreigners you will be meeting? Do they have sound bases or should you discuss them?
- 'Visitors' may, in some contexts, be a more appropriate description than 'foreigners'.

Effective Purchasing

This checklist is designed to assist those responsible for purchasing to adopt a more effective strategy. It is not intended that this checklist should itemise the steps in the administration of a purchase order process; rather it is aimed at presenting a proactive approach to purchasing. Whilst directed at those involved in centralised purchasing, the principles apply equally to decentralised buying.

MCI Standards

This checklist has relevance for the MCI Management Standards: Key Role B – Manage Resources.

Definition

Most textbooks advocate that purchasing is about buying the right goods, at the right time, at the right price, in the right quantity and of the right quality. Whilst this is indeed a fundamental requirement, effective purchasing has to deliver more than this. Adopting an effective purchasing strategy will turn a reactive buyer into a proactive buyer, one who adds value to the process.

Advantages of effective purchasing

It:

- is proactive and adds value for your organisation
- improves communication with suppliers
- provides better understanding of the marketplace.

Disadvantages of effective purchasing

There are no real disadvantages to effective purchasing, but it must be remembered that time must be invested in:

- gathering and sorting internal data
- evaluating suppliers.

Action checklist – Your organisation

1. Understand your own organisation

Take time to learn about how your own organisation functions and what is important to each department in terms of the supply of goods and services. What are the most crucial aspects for each line manager in terms of quality, price and delivery? Which items do they purchase most often and what are they used for? How does each department determine its re-order levels? Gather as much data as you can to provide a sound basis for formulating your strategy. It will also serve to demonstrate professionalism to your internal customers and increase their sense of involvement in the process.

2. Compile a purchase history

Use purchase orders and requisitions to compile a history of purchases. Gather data on product types, order quantities, lead times, pricing, order frequency, etc. Use this data to produce a pattern of purchasing for key items.

3. Use the purchase history to become a proactive buyer

Negotiate better deals with suppliers by giving them an indication of the volumes they can expect over the year. Anticipate re-order dates and do the groundwork in advance. Reduce delivery charges by ordering like products at the same time. Arrange for suppliers to stock frequently used items free of charge, thus reducing your storage requirements, controlling lead times and giving the benefit of bulk purchasing. Monitor price fluctuations for seasonal trends.

Action checklist – Your suppliers

1. Evaluate potential suppliers

Check:

- turnover and profitability
- how long they have been trading
- who their major customers are (if they are reliant on one major customer what will happen to the business if they lose that account?)
- what percentage of their turnover your business will generate
- whether they have any third party certification, such as ISO 9000
- their quality control policy
- their procedure for handling customer complaints
- their invoicing and administrative procedures
- their level of insurance cover.

2. Visit potential suppliers

Find out who would be dealing with your order and how it would be processed. Ask to meet the people with whom you will have day-to-day contact. Are you made to feel welcome?

3. Assess supplier competence

Take up references. Try to talk to buyers in organisations which are similar to your own with similar accounts.

4. Audit your major suppliers

Perform regular audits on your suppliers to assess their continued level of performance. Do they still meet the criteria you established when placing the first order? What improvements have you noticed in the service since then?

5. Maintain good communication

You expect your suppliers to keep you advised of delivery dates and any problems associated with your order. Ensure that you reciprocate – advise them if you are expecting a sudden decrease in purchases or indeed an increased requirement. Just as you should tell them exactly what you want of them, get them to tell you precisely what they expect of you.

Show an interest in your supplier's other business. Have they won or lost any major contracts? How are they affected by the economy? Will transport costs increase as a result of rising fuel prices? Will the price of paper materially affect your major print job scheduled for the end of the year – can you pre-purchase the paper to minimise the effect? Good communication and understanding of your supplier's business will ultimately filter back into your own.

Get to know your suppliers as human beings. It is much easier to deal with matters (especially tricky ones) when you know the person at the other end of the phone (but don't let personal considerations outweigh organisational ones).

6. Use your supplier's expertise

You cannot be an expert in everything. Use your supplier's expertise and knowledge to help you draw up specifications of work.

7. Maintain a competitive element

Always review the price and service you are getting from your supplier. Let them know they have to remain competitive. For audit purposes retain documentation which shows you sought alternative prices.

8. Compare quotations

Ensure quotes are based on a level playing field. Check the exclusions such as delivery, installation, training and insurance. Check the contract period, renewal dates and how long the price is held for. What provision is made to hold prices at current level or within the realms of RPI for long-term contracts? What are the payment terms?

9. Visit trade exhibitions

Visiting trade exhibitions and reading trade journals are fundamental to keeping up-to-date with the marketplace and what is on offer.

10. Negotiate when the price must rise

Try to negotiate other advantages, such as longer payment terms, prompt payment discounts, quarterly invoicing (as opposed to monthly), management reports, price stability for a fixed period, free delivery or increased delivery frequency. Remember, the supplier wants to maintain your business and may be able to help in other ways.

Action checklist – General hints/good practice

1. Establish a code of ethics

- Respect confidentiality – do not disclose suppliers' prices and methods of trading to competitors.
- Declare any personal interest.
- Do not accept gifts from suppliers or potential suppliers (it is good practice to advise all suppliers of this in writing when you commence trading with them and prior to the Christmas period when most suppliers traditionally bear gifts!).

2. Beware

- If you have a roll-over contract, make sure you know when you have to give notice should you wish to terminate.
- Be aware of authority limits and do not exceed your authority.
- Never make assumptions – ensure all details are clarified in writing.

3. Fulfil your side of the contract

Ensure payment is made in accord with your agreement.

4. Maintain an audit trail

Always maintain an audit trail of all purchase documents.

Dos and don'ts for effective purchasing

Do

- Involve your internal customers in the purchasing process.
- Assess and visit your suppliers regularly.
- Build relationships with suppliers based upon mutual trust and good communication.
- Establish a clear code of ethics.

Don't

- Allow yourself to be dragged into a 'Dutch auction' by your suppliers.
- Stay with the same supplier 'because you've always used them' – be sure you're using them 'because they're the best'.

Useful reading

Managing purchasing: sourcing and contracting, Andrew Erridge, Oxford: Butterworth-Heinemann, 1995

Successful purchasing in a week, Stephen Carter, London: Hodder & Stoughton, 1995

Buying business equipment and services: a management guide, Kingston upon Thames: Croner Publications, 1995, Amendment service available by annual subscription.

Are you managing purchasing: a guide to better buying, Malcolm Jones, London: Nicholas Brealey Publishing, 1992

Purchasing: principles and applications, 7th ed, Stuart F Heinritz, Paul V Farrell and Clifton L Smith, Englewood Cliffs, NJ: Prentice-Hall, 1986

Useful address

Chartered Institute of Purchasing and Supply, Easton House, Easton on the Hill, Stamford, Lincolnshire PE9 3NZ, Tel: 01780 56777

Thought starters

- How much do you know about your organisation's annual purchases?
- What is your organisation's annual spend with each of its major suppliers?
- How often have you visited your major suppliers?

Stock Control

This checklist deals with some of the main principles involved in the practice of stock control, as it was traditionally called, or inventory control as it has become more widely known.

Stock control is important at both ends of a spectrum. Too much stock of the wrong kind – or even the right kind – means that cash resources are tied up unnecessarily, that cash flow is prejudiced and that, in extreme cases, survival may be in jeopardy. Too little stock of the right kind threatens prosperity and growth if the result is that an adequate level of resource cannot be provided to customers, internal or external, or clients. Whilst stock control is therefore very important, it is also often the subject of neglect.

This checklist is not a manual on stock control. It highlights lines of enquiry for the manager who wishes to raise the standards of stock control in their business.

MCI Standards

This checklist has relevance for the MCI Management Standards: Key Role B – Manage Resources.

Definition

Stock control is the sum total of the policies, practices and procedures which an organisation should follow to ensure that its stocks are at levels which are, on the one hand, consistent with meeting predetermined standards of services and, on the other, consistent with releasing funds for the purposes of working capital rather than inhibiting cash flow, its life blood.

Stocks are held by retailers (finished goods), wholesalers (finished goods), manufacturers (finished goods, part finished goods, parts, and raw materials), local authorities (a range of stocks for use), other public bodies (likewise), indeed every type of organisation.

For the purposes of this checklist, strategic stock is defined as stock without which the organisation cannot function, ie essential stock.

Non-strategic stock is defined as basic commodities, not critical to the overall function of the organisation, which can be readily sourced.

Benefits of stock control

Whilst effective practice in stock control requires the application of significant effort and resources to introduce a system which offers maximum advantage at a reasonable cost, it also:

- ensures that cash is released for the major purposes for which the organisation exists
- ensures that the standard of service is consistent with predetermined policy
- ensures that stockholding costs (the cost of finance; storage; insurance; handling; obsolescence; pilferage) are minimised.

Action checklist

1. Recognise the steps necessary to achieve control of stocks

Stock control can be extremely simple, from ledger books and card index systems to highly computerised operating environments.

Establish a system which will provide a knowledge of current stocks on a regular basis and a system which will record supplies received and sales, deliveries, outputs and usage. Develop a system which is not based on precise stock records for every item held. The system adopted will depend on common sense – the cost of the system and its operation must not be greater than the cost of the problem which it is intended to solve. However, the following steps must be built into any stock control system:

- identification of current stock levels
- recording of receipts/dispatches
- identification of re-order levels and quantities (by analysing lead times, volume discounts, price stability) – recognise that this has a cost in itself in the form of higher ordering costs, loss of bulk discounts, and perhaps additional handling charges
- establishment of a pattern of regular auditing and stock checking.

2. Analyse usage

Analyse usage of all items in terms of:

- volume
- strategic/non-strategic stock.

It is important to:

- recognise key products which must be available on demand and 'be right' first time
- classify products in terms of importance to overall turnover but not in big product families or in other broad product groupings

- focus attention on the items which produce the most revenue
- avoid trying to give equal attention to all stock items
- analyse sales to identify the real money earners and recognise that 50% will probably yield only 10% of the total value.

Identify the level of stock which must be held to avoid the risk of missing core opportunities or failing to supply basic needs. Identify non-strategic stock and reduce it by:

- special offers
- non-replacement
- repackaging
- scrapping for salvage value

and, in extreme cases

- writing it off.

Don't spend time monitoring products which yield 5-10% of annual revenue – reduce your stocks of them. Monitor the right 20% and achieve control over 80% of total stock values. Avoid making arbitrary demands to reduce stocks by X% – to do so may result in reduced service levels without identifying areas of wasted investment.

Identify the level of stock above which excess inventory ties up money and diminishes the return on capital employed.

3. Plan your stocking area

- Locate frequently used items in an accessible place.
- Train staff in methods of handling – manual handling and operation of mechanical handling equipment.
- Choose appropriate stacking methods – consider pallets, drums, bins, shelving, pipe racks. Do not try to store every item in the same environment.
- Consider shelf life and implement a stock rotation system.
- Consider storing large or bulky items at your suppliers if you have insufficient space – ensure availability meets requirements.
- Use an appropriate labelling system for stock identification (this might include bar coding or a simple handwritten label).
- Consider environmental conditions, such as temperature and humidity.

4. Establish appropriate resourcing

Don't underestimate, in terms of numbers or quality, staff required for running your stock control system – too few and you will lose control of your stocks, too many and the cost of running your stock control system will be prohibitive.

5. Identify the cost of stockholding

Discover (if any):

- financial costs (the cost of funds or lost opportunities for better investment)
- storage costs, including equipment and labour costs
- costs of protection from damp, cold or damage
- insurance costs
- handling costs
- costs of obsolescence
- cost of losses through pilferage
- the alternative rental value of your storage facilities.

6. Adopt a common sense approach

You cannot control every item by quantity – you would not expect someone to count out paperclips or screws. Consider classifying such items as consumables and make the conscious decision not to count these items. Some lines may be controlled by weight.

7. Build links to other departments

Try to develop a system which links through to other departments. A system which works hand in hand with the accounts department will minimise workloads for both sections. Good communication with buyers and dispatch departments will minimise the risk of staff and plant being overworked one day and then having little to do the next.

Dos and don'ts for stock control

Do
- Recognise that in a well-run organisation stock levels are planned.
- Think of stock as money.
- Relate stocks to known or anticipated sales, deliveries, demand or usage.
- Consider whether you are carrying excessive stock.
- Establish, and review regularly, re-order levels and re-order quantities.
- Ensure that one official in your organisation is made responsible for coordinating the output of stock, output forecasts, purchasing and stock control.

Don't
- Assume that you aren't suffering from pilferage, excessive waste or some other form of 'shrinkage'.
- Exaggerate the potential consequences of 'running out'.
- Grab every quantity or early delivery discount offered, assuming that it is to your advantage.

- Let stock-taking become an annual nightmare – do it regularly on a partial basis.
- Think that a stock control system must be expensive and complex – a basic system may give you the control which is lacking now, at a cost below the resulting savings.
- Hold stocks only to fill the store or warehouse.
- Buy speculatively or to obtain quantity discounts or to qualify for early delivery concessions.

Useful reading

Storage and supply of materials: inbound logistics for commerce and industry and public undertakings, 6th ed, David Jessop and Alex Morrison, London: Pitman, 1994
Principles of inventory and materials management, 4th ed, Richard H Tersine, Englewood Cliffs NJ: Prentice Hall, 1994
Inventory control and management, C D J Waters, Chichester: John Wiley, 1992

Thought starters

- Who really controls our stock levels?
- You lock the safe carefully because it contains £100. How much thought do you give to the warehouse which contains stock worth £250,000?

Taking Action on the Environment

This checklist is designed as an aid to the development of an action plan to comply with environmental regulations.

The environment has come to the forefront of industrial and commercial decision-making in recent years. The onus, and liability, is increasingly on senior managers and directors to come to terms with environmental responsibilities by adopting an environmental policy and initiating an action plan.

This checklist is therefore aimed primarily at senior managers who have, or will have, responsibility for tackling environmental issues.

MCI Standards

This checklist has relevance for the MCI Management Standards: Key Roles A, B and E – Manage Activities, Manage Resources and Manage Energy.

Definition

An environmental action plan brings together the key elements of environmental management, including:

- the organisation's policy statement
- the environmental audit
- environmental management systems and standards including the **EC ECO-Management Audit Scheme (EMAS)** and **ISO 14001: Environmental management systems**
- setting targets and measuring performance against them
- identifying key responsibilities to set the system in motion

and places them in a sequential order for action.

Advantages

An environmental action plan will:

- demonstrate commitment to customers, shareholders and legislators that action to reduce damage to the environment is a priority
- provide a coherent statement of policy and a practical system for implementation
- lead to reduced waste and cost
- lead to closer examination of processes and raw materials which can contribute to cost savings and improved productivity
- help to develop improved communications and management systems through better information on sources of environmental impacts
- lay a foundation for effective management of environmental risk.

Disadvantages

- Staff may not see the need to change.
- Stakeholders may only see the costs as opposed to an investment which will yield benefits.
- Benefits may be slow to accrue while costs are quickly incurred.

Action checklist

1. Gain top management commitment

Make sure that the implications of good – and bad – environmental practice are fully understood by top managers and key stakeholders.

2. Designate a senior manager

Allocate responsibility for environmental matters at senior level.

3. Identify environmental laws and regulations

Do your homework on relevant legislation and codes of practice – liability usually means that the polluter pays.

4. Consider whether to apply for registration under ISO 14001 or EMAS

Registration provides a recognised framework for environmental management and may give competitive advantage where there is a need to demonstrate conformance.

5. Review the environmental impact of your organisation's operations

This will enable you to determine the issues which need to be addressed.

6. Work out the environment–business link

Focus on issues where environmental improvements can be directly related to financial and quality targets: for example, the generation of new or improved product lines through recycling waste, or the justification of price increases for more environmentally desirable products.

7. Establish your policy

Draw up a clear statement which covers objectives, improvement programmes, audits, supplier and customer liaison, compliance with standards, and responsibility to the community.

8. Build in measures and records

These should cover not only outputs (damage to, or impact on, the environment) and inputs (damage created by raw materials), but also process measures (pollution created by out-of-date or worn-out machinery). Keep detailed records – legislation and ISO 14001 may require evidence of conformance.

9. Develop a procedures manual

The manual should be a 'who does what and how' of operational control achieved through work instructions, performance criteria, measurements, tests and verification.

10. Launch an environmental training programme

Build the environment into routine operational practice. The organisation will benefit from environmental goals being integrated with financial, personal and operational targets.

11. Involve your employees

Work on the commitment of staff by involving them directly rather than issuing remote instructions. Publicise the objectives and targets which have been set.

12. Conduct regular audits

Use audits to see how things are going, correct what is going wrong and publicise what is going right.

13. Communicate environmental benefits internally and externally

Where possible, express environmental benefits in terms of financial savings. The promotion of direct community benefits can also enhance the organisation's image and reputation.

Dos and don'ts for environmental action

Do

- Try to spread the environmental message far and wide in the organisation; action will follow more easily.
- Ensure that staff receive appropriate information and training.
- Focus attention on all stages of the product life-cycle not just the end.
- Take account of environmental policies of suppliers, customers and competitors.
- Communicate what you are doing to the outside world.

Don't

- Wait for legislation, or bad press, to force you to act.
- Impose complicated systems without full consultation and feedback.
- Assume the environment is irrelevant if you are not in manufacturing.
- Equate measurement and records with bureaucracy – if it gets measured it gets done.
- Ignore ISO 14001.

Measuring Environmental Damage

1. Input measures will need to include indicators, targets and measures of plant efficiency, materials quality and recyclability, and effectiveness of training in operational procedures.
2. Process measures should aim at percentage improvements in reducing waste in manufacturing, finishing and packaging.
3. Output measures record impact on, or damage to, the community and should measure reductions in waste or pollution discharge. Output measures are those which relate most to the organisation's image and reputation and are the ones most likely to be reported outside the organisation.

Useful reading

BOOKS

Corporate environmental management: systems and strategies, Richard Welford (ed),
London: Earthscan, 1996

ISO14000: a guide to the new environmental management standards, Toni Tibor and Ira
Feldman, Chicago: Irwin, 1996

Blueprint for green management: creating your company's own environmental action plan,
George Winter, London: McGraw Hill, 1995

Environmental management handbook, Bernard Taylor and others, London: Pitman, 1994

JOURNAL ARTICLE

ISO 14000: the next focus in standardization, Amir M Hormozi, SAM Advanced
Management Journal, Vol 62 no 3, Summer 1997, pp32–41

STANDARD

ISO 14001: Environmental management systems – specification with guidance for use.
1996.

Useful addresses

Institute of Environmental Assessment, Welton House, Limekiln Way, Lincoln, LN2 4US,
Tel: 01522 540069

Institute of Environmental Management, 58-59 Timber Bush, Edinburgh, EH6 6QH, Tel:
0131 555 5334

UK Environmental Law Association, Cheapside House, 138 Cheapside, London, EC2V
1BB, Tel: 0171 551 7777

The Environment Council, 21 Elizabeth Street, London, SW1W 9RP, Tel: 0171 824 8411

Institute of Ecology and Environmental Management, 36 Kingfisher Court, Hambridge
Road, Newbury, Berks, RG14 5UP, Tel: 01635 37715

Council for Environmental Education, University of Reading, London Road, Reading,
Berks, RG1 5AQ, Tel: 01734 756061

British Standards Institute, 389 Chiswick High Road, London, W4 4AL, Tel: 0181 996
9000

Thought starters

- 'Businesses made a great deal of money fouling the world over the last
  200 years. I have no doubt that there are many fortunes to be made
  cleaning things up over the next three generations.' (Sir Crispin Tickell)
- Some 23 billion tonnes of carbon dioxide are pumped in to the earth's
  atmosphere every year.
- Tropical rainforests – the world's lungs – are being cut back by 170,000
  square kilometres per year.

Setting Up an Energy Management Scheme

This checklist provides guidance for those wishing to control the amount of energy consumed by their company or organisation.

Organisations are under increasing pressure to reduce costs and protect the environment. Energy can be costly and harm the environment. All organisations use it, and many see it as a 'fixed cost' that cannot be reduced. However, there are ways in which the amount of energy used can be reduced, leading to savings, and a successful energy management scheme can produce benefits both for the organisation and the environment.

MCI Standards

This checklist has relevance for the MCI Management Standards: Key Roles E and G – Manage Energy and Manage Projects.

Definition

An energy management scheme provides a systematic and continuous method of assessing, improving and evaluating an organisation's energy usage.

Advantages of an energy management scheme

An effective energy management scheme:

- saves money
- conveys an 'environmentally friendly' attitude
- often makes for greater employee workplace comfort.

Disadvantages of an energy management scheme

There are no real disadvantages to introducing an energy management scheme, but remember that it takes time and can require initial expenditure to accrue long-term savings or environmental benefits.

Action checklist

1. Designate an Energy Management Committee

The members of the Energy Management Committee should be drawn from all levels of the organisation. Members from the finance and purchasing departments should be included, together with the transport manager where applicable. The Committee will manage the assessment, improvement and evaluation of energy usage. Appoint a coordinator (someone with project management experience who commands respect and can get things done) to oversee the scheme. If expertise or resources available are limited consider calling in an energy management consultant.

2. Define the scope and coverage of the scheme

Depending on the size of the organisation it is advisable to concentrate on one building or site initially; the experiences from this can then be used to improve energy efficiency throughout the rest of the organisation. It may also be decided to look at only one type of energy usage, for example, heating or use of company vehicles.

3. Gather information

Ask the committee's finance department representative to produce a report of all the energy bills over the last couple of years. Check the tariffs being paid. Do they look sensible, or too high? Look for variations in consumption over the year.

Contact the local Energy Efficiency Office to ascertain whether any grants are available for your organisation. The Office should also be able to provide figures giving best practice energy usage which can be compared with those of your organisation. If possible, try to compare your organisation's energy usage figures with those of another organisation.

4. Undertake an energy audit

This involves an examination of the organisation to highlight energy wastage. Checklists should be produced covering different areas.

Areas to cover and points to look for include:

- Transport
  - Are vehicles properly serviced, maintained and tuned?
  - Do employees share vehicles when they are travelling to the same place on business?
  - Do some drivers appear to use too much fuel? Do they need instruction in fuel economy?
  - Is the most cost-effective form of transport used?

- Lighting
  - Are the most efficient light bulbs being used?
  - Could more use be made of daylight by moving workstations nearer windows?
  - Are lights switched off when rooms are not in use?

- Heating
  - Is the heating system serviced regularly?
  - Are thermostats functioning correctly and are they set to the correct temperature?
  - Is the heating switched off or turned down when the building is empty?

- Air conditioning
  - Is there really a need for it?
  - Is the system kept clean and regularly maintained?
  - Is it working against the heating system?

- Insulation
  - Are the wall and roof insulation materials of the correct type and thickness?

- Ventilation
  - Do employees open doors or windows to cool the place down rather than turning down thermostats?
  - Are there excessive draughts from badly fitting doors and windows?

- Equipment / machinery
  - Is machinery running efficiently?
  - Could any heat / energy produced by processes be re-used?
  - Is the right size of machine used for each job?
  - Are computers turned off when not in use?

Every member of the Committee should be involved in the preparation and carrying out of the survey. It can be split by department or site, or each member can look at one particular aspect of energy use.

5. Analyse the results and make improvements / modifications

The results of the survey should highlight areas where action can be taken immediately (for example turning down thermostats) and areas where investment may be needed to produce long-term gains (for example a more efficient boiler system). Ensure that the purchasing department takes energy efficiency into account when making acquisitions by asking suppliers about the energy consumption of any machinery or equipment to be purchased. Ask the department to look for more energy-efficient machines that could replace the present ones cost-effectively, and new innovations such as systems that switch off lights automatically unless deliberately reactivated.

One of the most essential actions is to implement a system of regular servicing and maintenance of heating equipment and machinery, where one is not already in place.

Keep a record of all the changes made, so that improvements in energy usage can be monitored.

6. Communicate and train staff

Communicate the benefits of reduced costs through improved energy management to all employees. Provide training on ways in which workers can reduce energy usage, for example, by not opening windows to cool down an office but turning the heating down. The checklists used to undertake the energy audit will help with this. Ask suppliers to provide training on the best ways to maintain and service specialist equipment. Reward staff who suggest successful ways in which energy usage can be reduced.

7. Evaluate the changes and look for further improvements

Check the energy bills after the scheme has been implemented and record any reductions. Communicate successes to all employees. Hold regular meetings of the Energy Management Committee to look for further ways in which energy usage can be reduced.

Dos and don'ts for an energy management scheme

Do
- Make maintenance and servicing a regular process.
- Let all staff know of the importance of reducing energy usage.
- Ensure purchasing staff look at energy efficiency before making an acquisition.

Don't
- Forget to record the amount spent on energy before the scheme is implemented.
- Hide the results of the scheme – inform all staff of its success.
- Stop after one audit and set of responses – continually look for improvements.

Useful reading

Books

Energy management: good for business, good for the environment, London: Confederation of British Industry, 1993

Practical energy saving guide for smaller businesses: save money and help the environment, London: Energy Efficiency Office, 1992

101 ways to improve energy efficiency, Peter Heslop, Newmarket: Energy Publications, 1984

JOURNAL ARTICLES

Heating: how to balance the cost and comfort, Roy Holder Works Management, Vol 48 no 10, October 1995, pp61, 63, 65

Why energy efficiency is so smart, Andrew Warren, Director, Vol 48 no 11, June 1995, pp76, 79–80

Energy efficiency measures for small firms, National Westminster Bank Small Business Digest, April 1991, pp1–5

Useful addresses

Details of local Energy Efficiency Offices may be obtained from:

Environment and Energy Management Directorate, 2 Marsham Street, London, SW1P 3EB, Tel: 0171 276 3706

Thought starters

- Do you make sure all lights are switched off when you leave the office?
- Are all the radiators functioning correctly?
- Does your company car use too much petrol?

Planning the Replacement of Software Systems

This checklist is a starting-point for those who have to replace an out-dated or inadequate software package with a new one.

There will be numerous reasons for changing software packages, key among them the need for increased flexibility, integration with other systems, greater employee productivity and improved customer service. Costings should cater for data conversion, customisation, installation and training, and the adoption licence as well as the package itself. Although you may wish to form a small working party, consult staff throughout the selection process, including those who will have to use the system and senior staff with line and budget responsibility.

MCI Standards

This checklist has relevance for the MCI Management Standards: Key Roles A, B, D and G – Manage Activities, Manage Resources, Manage Information and Manage Projects.

Action checklist

1. Establish objectives

Before contacting suppliers it is important to have a clear idea of priorities. These may change as the project unfolds and learning proceeds but it is vital to keep them firmly in mind. A checklist of firm requirements should start to emerge from answering questions such as the following.

- How does your current package hinder customer service improvements and flexibility for future developments?
- How does your current package impede integration?
- Are other systems within the organisation going to be renewed?
- Who is going to use the package and how?
- What degree of independence from the supplier is required?

- What degree of customisation and tailoring is required compared with an off-the-shelf, standard package?
- Must the package fit the existing hardware and operating system which you have?
- What improvements would you like to see from your old package?

2. Identify and exploit appropriate sources of suppliers

These include:

- suggestions from contacts, for example in similar organisations
- visits to exhibitions
- attendance at seminars and courses
- consulting directories and the trade and professional press
- using consultancy.

3. Establish a shortlist

Keep the checklist of requirements to hand and look at a number of systems. Decide which of these would be worth considering in detail. Try to match the size and capability of the package with the size of the organisation or department.

4. Send out the invitations to tender (ITT)

The ITT is a formal statement of your requirements sent to the suppliers on the shortlist, inviting them to reply with a formal proposal. It sets out a timetable for making a final selection and this should include visits to other users of the systems and to the offices of the suppliers. (ITTs are covered in the following checklist).

5. Select the package

Study each package in detail to ensure that the claims of the supplier can be substantiated and to check that it can meet your specific functional needs. Other questions concerning the package in general, the supplier, support and training will need to be addressed.

The package

- How old is it? Does it offer all that the present system offers?
- Is it modular?
- Are all modules easy to use? Are all modules compatible?
- Is it capable of data exchange? Receiving? Downloading?
- Can it integrate with a word processing package? With other packages within the organisation?
- How often is it upgraded?
- What are the future plans for the package?
- What operating systems does it run on?

- How is it updated? Realtime? Batch?
- What is the system of backups?
- How many concurrent users can it support?
- How many installations are there? In the UK? In Europe? In the US?
- Can you visit other user sites, particularly migrations?
- What problems have other users encountered? How quickly were they resolved? How do the users react to the supplier and to the package?
- What are the capital and start-up costs?

Support

- How long has the supplier been operating?
- Is the supplier financially sound?
- Can the supplier support all modules?
- What is the cost of maintenance per annum?
- Do customer support costs appear to be value for money?
- Does the supplier offer on-site or dial-up support?
- How much support is given prior to migration?
- How much work is left to the customer?
- How is the helpdesk organised?

Training

- Does the supplier offer training as part of the fee?
- Is pre-conversion training available?
- Can you hire a machine to train on in advance?

Migration

- What is the size of the migration team?
- What are the skills of the supplier's migration staff?
- Is the conversion process tried and tested?
- How many data migrations has the supplier performed?
- Can you have a trial data conversion?
- Is there enough contingency time planned to allow for mistakes?

6. Scrutinise the contract terms

Look carefully at the responsibilities and liabilities of the supplier and question any term which may be open to misinterpretation. Include in the contract details of any modifications which you want made to the package and specify any tests you want run before you accept it. Question the level of support and after sales service detailed in the contract and check that the final costs cover all aspects of the purchase, including items like delivery and training.

7. Plan for implementation

Once you have chosen a package, a further objective will be to minimise the disruption of services on conversion to a new system. Ways to do this include:

- running trial data conversions
- having a period of parallel running
- training from the supplier for all staff or for the trainer
- choosing the timing carefully, for example, not at peak holiday times
- managing modifications to the package.

8. Manage the 'people' side

From the start to the finish of the project, ensure close involvement with staff who will have to use the system.

- Who is coordinating the views, reactions and progress of staff?
- Who is checking that current and developing operational needs are being satisfied?
- Who is coordinating the emerging – as opposed to prescribed – training requirements?

Dos and don'ts for replacing software systems

Do

- Plan site visits where the package is up and running.
- Check out undemonstrated or unsubstantiated claims of the supplier.
- Set up a team of users and consult widely.
- See the products of at least 4–5 suppliers before shortlisting.
- Be wary of too much 'bespoke' work on 'your' application.

Don't

- Take what the supplier says for granted.
- Make assumptions about what is stated or not stated by the supplier.
- Focus too much on your current application.
- Neglect the importance of forward-thinking.
- Let the supplier deter you from your objectives.
- Forget to build in adequate contingency time.
- Skip 'apparently' minor details.

Useful reference/reading material

Computer Users Yearbook, London: Learned Information, annual

Software Users Yearbook, London: Learned Information, annual

Crash: ten easy ways to avoid computer disaster, Tony Collins and David Bicknell, London: Simon and Schuster, 1997

Thought starters

- How old is your current package?
- How often is it upgraded?
- How much bespoke work does your current package include?
- How long is it since you took a good look at alternative packages?
- How good is your current support desk?

Writing an Invitation to Tender

This checklist focuses on the process of writing an invitation to tender by detailing what should be included in the invitation document.

When purchasing capital equipment there are various steps that you can take to ensure that a cost-effective solution, matched as far as possible to your particular needs, is reached. Having made sure that your objectives conform to your organisation's overall strategy, specified a statement of requirements and drawn up a short list of suppliers, you can then invite suppliers to tender.

MCI Standards

This checklist has relevance for the MCI Management Standards: Key Role D – Manage Information.

Definition

An invitation to tender (ITT) is a formal document which asks suppliers to demonstrate that they can meet your requirements. Each supplier, if they wish to respond to the invitation, should respond with a formal proposal.

Advantages of writing an ITT

- Clarifies the issues involved and makes sure nothing is left out.
- Provides a standard against which to assess the tenders received.

Action checklist

When drafting the ITT ensure that the following points are included.

1. Set the scene

This summarises the purpose and content of the document and defines the objectives. The conditions attached to a response should be stated; for example, you will probably stipulate that suppliers should keep the ITT document confidential and should not pass on any costs incurred in replying to it. Enclose a pre-paid label and request that the envelope containing the quote does not identify the supplier. Give clear instructions about deadlines.

2. Provide background information

To give the suppliers a perspective on your organisation, a description of its mission and activities should be included here. This section may also give additional, more specific information such as physical / environmental considerations or constraints, and longer term objectives. An invitation to visit the site should be extended where appropriate.

3 List the main applications or functions required

More detailed requirements should be placed in the statement of requirements in an appendix. You must make clear what is essential and what is desirable. The evaluation process will be much more difficult if you allow the tenderers to assume your needs.

4. Estimate usage volumes

The amount of traffic or usage that the package will have to cope with should be estimated and future growth predicted. The number of present and future users should be estimated in order for suppliers to provide quotes on any necessary licences. Think about long-term requirements; will there be an increase or decrease in the usage of the capital equipment?

5. Set time scales

This section should include the following elements:

a) issue of ITT (and return date)
b) clarification discussions with shortlisted suppliers
c) presentation by shortlisted suppliers of how they can meet your requirements
d) evaluation of responses
e) final negotiations
f) presentation from preferred supplier or the selection team to senior management
g) contract awarded.

All suppliers should be given an opportunity to ask for clarification of any issue raised in the document. Copies of questions and answers should be circulated to all suppliers.

6. Detail requirements

Details of the precise general and functional requirements of the organisation should be included in appendices. The general requirements may take the form of a questionnaire and will cover:

- registered and trading offices
- insurance details
- trading record
- employment data, including staff turnover and an organisational chart
- health and safety policies
- quality policies
- environmental policies.

Specific requirements will cover:

- the supplier
- the package
- implementation and support
- maintenance
- performance
- price.

The statement of functional requirements should be the result of agreement between users on their detailed needs. It should take the form of a numbered list for ease of comparison between suppliers and should not invite subjective evaluations or assertions. It is useful to specify that the response to each requirement must be coded:

A – Meets requirement
B – Simple modification required
C – Major modification required

Explain that if the suppliers wish to give additional information, they should accompany it with the requirement reference number. An indication of the time allowed by the organisation to each supplier to discuss the ITT and their response may be included.

Assessing responses to the ITT

The timetable set in the ITT should be strictly adhered to in fairness to the suppliers. Examine the written, formal responses to the ITT in conjunction with evidence you have gleaned from demonstrations, discussions and visits to other users: it is dangerous to rely on one source of information only.

Dos and don'ts for writing ITTs

Do

- Be clear on what you want to achieve.
- Involve all stakeholders in drawing up the statement of requirements.
- Stick to the timetable.
- Check whether any developments are planned by the supplier which might affect your choice or implementation programme.

Don't

- Take on trust the suppliers' answers to the ITT.
- Expect a perfect solution – you may have to select the best compromise.

Useful reading

BOOKS

Public procurement contracts, Euan Temple and Charles Bright, Kingston-upon-Thames: Croner Publications, 1994

Successful bidding and tendering, P D V Marsh, Aldershot: Wildwood House, 1989

JOURNAL ARTICLES

Balancing act, Brian Clark, Supply Management, vol 3 no 6, 26 March 1998, p43

10 proposal related questions customers should be prepared to answer, Paul Bernard, IIE Solutions, July 1997, pp34–38

CCTA model agreements for buying information systems and services, Paul Humphries, Purchasing and Supply Management, April 1994, pp13–17

Useful addresses

Chartered Institute of Purchasing and Supply, Easton House, Easton on the Hill, Stamford, Lincs PE9 3NZ, Tel: 01780 56777

Computer Services and Software Association, 73–74 High Holborn, London WC1V 6LE, Tel: 0171 405 2171

Thought starters

- How are you going to communicate all your requirements to suppliers?
- On what basis are you going to evaluate their replies?
- How much time do you have available?
- How many people should be involved in the process and at what level?

Implementing IT Software Solutions

This checklist aims to identify the key stages for the successful implementation of IT software solutions. It is designed for both IT professionals and end users.

MCI Standards

This checklist has relevance for the MCI Management Standards: Key Roles B, D and G – Manage Resources, Manage Information and Manage Projects.

Definition

Software solutions can largely be categorised as:

- bespoke programs and systems (commissioned with or without hardware)
- a software package which is heavily parameterised or customised for a particular type of client's needs (such as payroll or accounts systems)
- software which is embedded in hardware dedicated to one application (a dedicated word processor for example), sometimes known as turnkey systems
- proprietary off-the-peg programs (PC packages for word processing or spreadsheets for example).

This checklist is intended to deal primarily with the first two categories, and is also aimed principally at software provided by an external vendor rather than internally developed solutions.

Implementation should be seen as a key stage within an overall project. The purpose of implementation is to take a finished software product and make it fully operational in a live environment in such a way that users of the software are fully trained and receptive to its introduction and the intended objectives of the organisation are fully met with minimum disruption.

Implementation cannot be viewed in isolation. This checklist assumes that the process of defining requirements, supplier selection, tender issue, selection and verification of hardware platform and operating environment have, where appropriate, already been successfully completed.

Action checklist

1. Appoint a project manager

Even the smallest of software implementation projects should have a project manager. In larger projects the project manager might be responsible to a senior management project review board or an overall projects programme controller. The project manager will need to work closely with the software supplier and the appointed user group. So if you haven't already appointed someone to carry out this responsibility, do it now!

2. Set up a user group

A key component of any software implementation is the formation of a user group which should play an active role in determining the acceptability of any new system. This will also help to accelerate the processes of learning, communication and problem identification and solving. This group should ideally be in place well before the implementation process commences and preferably be involved in the original software selection decision.

User involvement at all stages of the process should mean the finished product is more likely to match the true requirements of the user community. Don't impose new software on the intended users without their cooperation and involvement – technical implementation counts for nothing if the users are unaware of the intended benefits, untrained in the effective use of the system or disturbed by its impact.

3. Develop thorough and detailed implementation plans

Each stage of implementation should be identified in the implementation plan. The critical elements of the plan are:

- installation dates
- training/consultancy activities
- data transfer – electronic or manual?
- parallel running if required
- piloting the system if required
- ordering stationery
- documentation
- contingency plans in case of delays.

Each element of the plan should include a summary of activities covered by it, plus the names of those responsible for its implementation and the time allowed for it. Don't underestimate the resource effort and time required to implement any new software system (whatever the software vendors say!). Failure will result in a mad scramble with corners being cut or a series of demoralising delays.

The implementation plan must formally culminate in implementation completion. At this point, the system passes out of the hands of the implementation team into the hands of the users and the operations and maintenance side of the IT function.

It is easy to forget the broader dimensions associated with software implementation which may impact on other systems, work procedures and organisational structure.

Prepare escalation procedures in the event of problems or delays in the project.

Review the plan regularly and report on the progress, usually weekly or monthly, but in extreme circumstances daily. Include the progress actually being made compared to the project plan and any issues or problems arising.

4. Ensure that there is adequate user documentation

Although it is usually the responsibility of the software provider to make documentation available with the software (either in printed or electronic form), this may not be appropriate for the users of the system. The project manager and the user group need to determine what user documentation should be delivered and at what stage as part of the implementation plan.

5. Review user procedures

New systems often result in changes to operational procedures. Failure to identify the extent of these changes or to agree and document the new procedures is one of the major causes of the failure of new systems even when the underlying software is quite sound. Also consider security and user access control for new systems and associated data.

6. Train and support all users

Consider what sort of training is required – in-house courses or external courses, manuals or tutorial packs for example – and the cost. Wherever possible include in the contract an agreement that the supplier will provide training. This should cover the cost of writing and distributing user manuals, running training courses and setting up a help desk.

7. Carry out proper software acceptance testing

Even with the most straightforward bespoke software development it is essential that there is a contractual framework for acceptance, which in turn should be linked to user testing and sign off. For larger software implementations it may be necessary to carry out the testing in phases. Ideally this should be linked to contractual payments to the software supplier. Also the consequences of failure to achieve acceptance should be stated in the contract.

8. Control the change process

Set up a Change Control mechanism to allow people to raise issues relating to the new software and for those issues to be properly assessed and resolved in an orderly and controlled manner. Remember that interfaces between the new software and other systems may need to be tested.

Don't allow software vendors to dictate terms/time scales for software implementation and acceptance. It must happen at a pace with which you feel comfortable and that the organisation can support.

9. Conduct a post-implementation review

For all except the smallest of software implementations, a post-implementation review is essential to determine whether the new software has satisfactorily achieved all of its stated objectives. This review should be carried out within a few months of implementation and should be wide-ranging in its approach.

Dos and don'ts for successful software implementation

Do

- Take a structured approach to implementing software.
- Ensure good communication between project staff, users and suppliers.
- Involve users at all stages of the process.
- Plan carefully.
- Carry out acceptance testing.

Don't

- Forget training and support.
- Underestimate the resources and time required.
- Impose a system on users – this will just add to your problems!
- Forget the impact new software can have on ways of working.

Useful reading

BOOK

How to implement information systems and live to tell about it, H Fallon, Chichester: John Wiley, 1995

JOURNAL ARTICLE

Selecting and implementing an accounting system 3: implementation, John Tate, Management Accounting, vol 74 no 7, Jul/Aug 1996, pp40–41

Useful addresses

British Computer Society, 1 Sanford Street, Swindon SN1 1HJ, Tel: 01793 417417
National Computing Centre, Oxford House, Oxford Road, Manchester M1 7ED, Tel: 0161 228 6333

Thought starters

- Have you been involved in a software implementation project before? What lessons can be learned from that experience?
- Did you cut corners to 'fit' the system?
- Did you get a picture of users' needs and user capability?

Implementing a Service Level Agreement

This checklist is for managers who need to draw up and implement a service level agreement. Although this checklist draws on examples from the Information Technology area, it may be used for agreements in any context.

There has been a surge of interest in Service Level Agreements (SLAs) with the growth of quality systems management, market testing and benchmarking. SLAs themselves have also grown in importance as a result of the evolution of the computer control function from Data Processing Department to Information Technology Services Centre.

The objective of an SLA is to improve the efficiency and effectiveness of the service provider for its customers through greater understanding of the needs and constraints of both sides and through greater account-ability.

The SLA may be of benefit not only to inter-departmental arrangements of both private and public sector organisations, but may also provide a valuable baseline for partnership and outsourcing arrangements.

MCI Standards

This checklist has relevance for the MCI Management Standards: Key Roles A and B – Manage Activities and Manage Resources.

Definition

Andrew Hiles defines an SLA as:

'an agreement between the provider of a service and its users which quantifies the minimum quality of service which meets the business need.'

Hiles stresses that this terminology is deceptively simple, in that:

- the agreement is the result of negotiation which recognises the needs and constraints on each side
- the agreement records and measures the level of service to which both parties subscribe as the requirement to meet needs

- the word 'minimum' implies 'adequate to meet quality needs' (those that serve the customer's needs and are acceptable to the customer).

Advantages of an SLA

Implementation of an SLA:

- serves to clarify understanding as the basis of meeting expectations
- makes the provider more accountable and responsible for the services delivered
- encourages the provider to plan for the development of services offered
- makes the user monitor and measure the efficiency and effectiveness of services from the provider
- makes the user more conscious of the costs of service provision
- makes the user plan ahead for services required
- should help to resolve difficulties in levels of user priority.

Disadvantages of an SLA

- An SLA can be seen as a threat by the provider.
- The provider may require extra resourcing to meet a minimum level of service acceptable and this could increase the cost of provision.
- It is not always easy to predict the level and nature of demand on the provider from all customers.

Action checklist

1. Assess the current situation of service provision

Most agreements do not start with a clean slate. They often arise because of past problems. It is as important for the user to define the minimum levels of service required as it is for the provider to assess its current – and planned – resources and the current and planned demand on them. It is at this stage that levels of urgency and priority may be defined.

2. Draw up an outline agreement

SLAs should identify at least the following elements:

- the purpose of the agreement
- the parties to the agreement, such as the provider and user of the service
- the service to be provided
- the period of the agreement, with notice if appropriate
- arrangements for monitoring, measuring and review

- the mechanism for resolving any conflicts
- the procedure(s) in case of non-performance (what happens if either party fails to meet the terms of the agreement?)
- procedures for change control
- the degree of contribution and help from the user
- lines of communication
- any charges, and insurance cover for both parties
- means of arbitration for unresolved disputes.

The key elements which both provider and user will need to clarify are:

- the precise nature of the service to be provided including timeliness, relevance, accuracy, format
- limits to the extent – scope, range and hours – of the service
- response times – expected and deliverable
- any exceptions to the rule
- agreed methods for monitoring and measuring.

3. Negotiate the levels of performance

The SLA will usually emerge from discussions between both parties in the form of a compromise which recognises the highest level of service feasible and the minimum that is acceptable. Although what constitutes 'unacceptable' service should be obvious to both parties, it is still worth mentioning to avoid possible misunderstandings. Equally, a 'top level' service should be discussed – what is desired may be impossible due to excessive costs.

The customer must clarify the levels of service required and response times. For example:

- **Priority 1:** must take precedence for immediate treatment
- **Priority 2:** requires treatment within the hour
- **Priority 3:** can wait for a maximum of 24 hours.

Another negotiation point will be any charges, or cross-charges for the services, penalties for failing to adhere to the agreement, and what to do in cases where disputes cannot be resolved by the two parties.

4. Include change control procedures

Information technology will be renewed at an ever faster pace. While this will impact on agreement targets and measures, it should also influence the nature of the agreement itself. The agreement must take account of changing hardware and software, and the continuity – and improvement – of services to the user during the transition phase.

Implemeting a Service Level Agreement

5. Consider contingency and back-up arrangements

Only in an ideal world can problems be solved in a flash and errors corrected at the touch of a button. The SLA must take account of this with due attention to risk management, which provides a measure of contingency and back-up (for example, for temporary operation of user services). Go a stage further with consideration of a disaster or crisis eventuality. Insurance may provide a warmth that things may be put right in time, but can it answer the immediacy that users normally require?

6. Measure performance and monitor faults

Agree a mechanism for monitoring and measuring the actual performance of the provider against the agreement. This may be in terms of speed or effectiveness as well as cost. Agreed performance targets or indicators (which should be precise) are useful here to provide a benchmark which will, in due course, indicate whether the existing levels of service are satisfactory or not.

7. Pilot the SLA first

The introduction of the SLA is important: lack of preparation or fine-tuning may well determine its fate. A sensible approach is to run an initial feasibility study with a pilot user group – not large enough to cause potential widespread damage if things go wrong, yet large enough to draw conclusions and make modifications for general implementation. It should be piloted by a user group with a clearly defined level of service need.

8. Review the SLA periodically

Resources, demands and targets will change over time; the SLA is not cast in stone and should be reviewed on at least an annual basis.

Measuring the effectiveness of SLAs

Records of speed of response, length of computer downtime and satisfaction with the solution can be rated against performance indicators agreed. The mean time between the failure and its repair/solution can provide an important indicator for the SLA. Response time can be reviewed against service objectives as agreed in the SLA.

Dos and don'ts for SLAs

Do

- Be ready to see the other person's point of view.
- Explore alternative service levels.
- Bear in mind the need to balance service against cost.
- Pay attention to detail during the initial assessment of requirements.
- Review the agreed performance indicators regularly.
- Recognise the resourcing and commitment required from both parties for success.
- Pay attention to definitions with a potential for disagreement, such as 'downtime' or 'availability'.

Don't

- Be satisfied with inadequate measurements.
- Accept cumbersome, ill-defined documentation.
- Ignore the cost of monitoring minimum quality service provision.
- Make the SLA too detailed or too difficult to monitor.
- Be satisfied with vague or impractical targets.

Useful reading

Service level agreements: measuring cost and quality in service relationships, Andrew Hiles, London: Chapman and Hall, 1993

Business planning in local government, John Delderfield, Ray Puffitt and Graham Watts, Harlow: Longman, 1991

Service level agreements, Alan Newton, Human Resources UK, no 23, March/April 1996, pp114–116

Service level agreements: panacea or pain, Andrew Hiles, TQM Magazine, vol 6 no 2, 1994, pp14–16

Getting outsourcing right, Harry Small, Business and Technology Magazine, September 1994, pp50–51

Service level agreements, Andrew Hiles, Payroll Managers Review, no 7, July 1989, pp70–71

Thought starters

- Is dissatisfaction with a central support service department frequent but not heard?
- How is your central support service provider monitored and evaluated?
- Does the proposed SLA use a sledge-hammer to crack a nut?

Implementing a Service Level Agreeement

Using Management Consulting Services Effectively

This checklist is for prospective users of consultants and suggests some of the questions they should ask themselves before approaching a consultant to undertake an assignment. There is little doubt that calling on the service of a management consultant can often prove to be a valuable investment provided:

● **you allow enough time for the whole exercise**

● **the problem area has been carefully defined**

● **you know what you want the consultant to do, having identified all the necessary steps for the task in hand**

● **care is exercised in selecting the right consultant**

● **you measure progress towards a solution.**

MCI Standards

This checklist has relevance for the MCI Management Standards: Key Role B – Manage Resources.

Definition

'*Management consulting is an advisory service contracted for and provided to organizations by specially trained and qualified persons who assist, in an objective and independent manner, the client organization to identify management problems, analyze such problems, recommend solutions to these problems, and help, when requested, in the implementation of solutions.*' **Consulting to management** by Larry E Greiner and Robert O Metzger, Prentice Hall 1983.

Advantages of using consultants

- **Expertise.** Since consultants are immersed in their specialism, they are well-placed to advise on the state of the art. It may be impossible for an organisation to tap such expertise in any other way.
- **Short-term projects.** It may be more cost-effective for a company to buy in skills as and when they are needed.
- **Extra resources.** Help can be required for an overstretched management team or to pursue a project that would otherwise not be completed.
- **Independent viewpoint.** An outsider can see things which are unclear to those on the inside or say things which members of staff may fear to articulate. Equally, employees may be more willing to agree to a course of action if they know that impartial advice has been taken.

Disadvantages of using consultants

- They may be expensive. The Management Consultancy Information Service (see Useful addresses) publishes regular surveys which give a guide to fee rates.
- The end result may be unsatisfactory although steps in the following action checklist will help you to guard against this.
- The work may be left to junior consultancy staff once the assignment starts or personnel may change during the project.
- There may be resentment from staff at the employment of consultants.

Action checklist

1. Involve senior management from the beginning

Gain their approval for the decision to use consultants and keep them informed during the selection process. This will help ensure that your choice of consultant will be accepted at the top level.

2. Gain an awareness of the number and scope of management consulting firms

Some offer a wide range of services, whilst there are others which specialise in particular industries, certain areas of business activity or smaller or larger organisations.

3. Prepare a short list of possible consultants

There are a number of directories and registers available for identifying consultants but recommendation is also commonly used. Make sure you obtain references from previous clients to establish a consultant's track record.

4. Ask for a preliminary survey from consultants on your short list

This should be free, although in certain circumstances a nominal charge may be made. It should enable you to establish the extent to which the consultant can help you, the likely benefits, and the duration of the job. It should also help you to study the consultant's approach to the problem and to your organisation. Ask for a written report of the survey.

5. Study the consultancy proposals submitted

These should have the following common features:

- an understanding of the situation or need
- a programme of work
- an indication of the consultant's management style and approach
- a timetable to accomplish the work
- details of staff involved, including relevant qualifications and experience
- the resources required, such as time, information and equipment
- estimates of fees and costs
- a summary of the results and benefits to be achieved from the project.

6. Explain to all concerned why a consultant is being employed

All relevant staff concerned must be fully briefed on why a consultant has been appointed, when he or she will arrive, and the cooperation that is required. Appoint someone as the main contact with the consultant.

7. Ask for regular reports on the progress of the assignment

Measure actual progress against the agreed objectives of the assignment. Ensure that your requirements are not being shrouded by consultant preferences.

8. Have a debriefing session before the end of the consultancy

Make sure the consultant summarises the findings and conclusions of the project either in a report or in a presentation. Ensure there are no misunderstandings or errors.

9. Assess consultant effectiveness

Check that the new development and procedures proposed are being implemented and properly applied, and that they are not being undermined by old methods and concepts. Discuss with staff concerned any particular difficulties which arise during implementation. Regularly examine the results being achieved and insist on follow-up visits from the consultant at appropriate intervals after completion of the project.

Dos and don'ts for using management consultants

Do

- Invest time in the whole process.
- Have a clear understanding of what you want to achieve.
- Prepare a checklist of requirements as a basis for reducing your short list to the final selection.
- Ensure effective communication and coordination between consultant and staff.

Don't

- Assume that you necessarily need to bring in an outsider.
- Accept friendly recommendations without investigating past performance.
- Presume that staff will readily accept an outside expert.
- Lose sight of your most important objectives.
- Become overly reliant on a consultant.

Useful reading

BOOKS

Directory of management consultants in the UK 1998, 13th ed, Alex Kaminsky, ed., London: AP Information Services, 1997
Getting the most from consultants: a manager's guide to choosing and using consultants, Martin Wilson and the Institute of Management Foundation, London: Pitman, 1996

JOURNAL ARTICLES

Using management consultants, IRS Employment Review, no 620, November 1996, pp7–12
The ten best ways of using management consultants, Geoff Kitts, Human Resources UK, no 15, Autumn 1994, pp19–20, 22, 24, 26
How to select an external consultant, Alan Fowler, Personnel Management Plus, vol 5 no 2, February 1994, pp26–27

Useful addresses

Institute of Management Consultants, 5th Floor, 32–33 Hatton Garden, London EC1N 8DL, Tel: 0171 242 2140; 0800 318030 (Client support service)
British Consultants Bureau, 1 Westminster Palace Gardens, 1–7 Artillery Row, London SW1P 1RJ, Tel: 0171 222 3651
Management Consultancies Association Ltd, 11 West Halkin Street, London SW1X 8JL, Tel: 0171 235 3897
Management Consultancy Information Service, 38 Blenheim Avenue, Gants Hill, Ilford, Essex IG2 6JQ, Tel: 0181 554 4695
All Business Links will provide help for those considering using a consultancy.

Thought starters

- Can you define clearly the problem or issue that needs to be tackled?
- Are you sure the expertise needed is not available internally?
- Have you worked with a consultant before? What was the outcome?

Total Quality: Mapping a TQM Strategy

This checklist provides guidance on mapping a strategy for total quality management (TQM) for those seeking to introduce TQM to the organisation for the first time. A quality strategy combines the 'hard' edge of quality (its tools and techniques) with its 'soft' side: the cultural changes you will need to achieve success. It is not just another management gimmick: it is a way of life.

The checklist is intended only as an aid to your initial thinking. Introducing TQM is a major strategic change which will require considerable research and planning. You are likely to need external advice or help to implement it.

MCI standards

This checklist has relevance for the MCI Management Standards: Key Role F – Manage Quality.

Definition

TQM is a style of managing which gives everyone in the organisation responsibility for delivering quality to the final customer, quality being described as 'fitness for purpose' or as 'delighting the customer'. TQM views each task in the organisation as fundamentally a process which is in a customer/supplier relationship with the next process. The aim at each stage is to define and meet the customer's requirements in order to maximise the satisfaction of the final consumer at the lowest possible cost.

Advantages of TQM

- It vastly improves the quality of the final product or service.
- There is a major decrease in wasted resources.
- There is a leap in productivity as staff use time more effectively.
- As products and services are improved, there should be a long-term increase in market share, leading to sustained competitive advantage.
- The workforce becomes more motivated, as employees realise their full potential.

Disadvantages of TQM

- It is extremely demanding of management and staff time.
- It can become overly bureaucratic and mechanical and lead to an emphasis on consistency rather than a focus on improvement, or the means rather than the end.
- It will only help if the organisation is heading in the right direction; it is not a tool for turning the organisation around.
- It is not a quick fix: TQM takes years to implement and is in fact an unending process.
- It can lead to too much attention being paid to the needs of final customers and not enough to those of employees.
- It is likely to cause perturbation at various stages and this has to be handled carefully.

Action checklist

1. Establish a planning team for total quality

You will need a quality team to drive through the changes. In a small organisation this will be the senior management team; in a larger one, it will comprise senior managers representing the major functions. Include in the team known sceptics or mavericks and ensure minority views are represented.

2. Assess the need to change

Consider the competitive position of the organisation. Establish who your key customers are and find out what they expect of you: don't assume that you are currently meeting all their requirements. Finding out what customers need is a continuous, not a one-off, process. Establish how other groups – suppliers, competitors and employees – view the quality of your product/service.

3. Define the vision

Draw up a vision statement defining where the organisation wants to be in terms of serving its customers: this vision must be stretching but attainable. Define the principles and values which underpin the vision. Use other organisations as a model but make sure your final draft reflects your own culture and circumstances.

4. Define the standard of service you aim to provide

Translate the vision into realistic outcomes. Establish what customers, suppliers and employees expect the organisation to deliver in quality of product/service.

5. Review how you are currently failing to meet the standards expected

There will often be a large gap between customer expectations and reality. Establish the reasons for this across the organisation. Key ones are: external constraints, being let down by suppliers and internal inefficiencies. It can happen that customers expect too little – you need to assess their needs, not only their overt wishes.

6. Conduct an organisational assessment of current levels of waste

Quantify the quality failures by securing from heads of departments an assessment of current levels of waste. Ensure they involve all employees in the assessment. Collect data as widely as possible, cost the results and present the findings to the senior management team.

7. Establish the current cost of waste

Work out how much is currently spent on rectifying internal failure (for example, reworking of below quality goods) and external failure (for example, handling customer complaints). Include appraisal costs – the time and money spent on inspection and checking.

8. Decide whether to go for third party certification

You need to decide whether to include a quality management system in your initiative. This will lead to third party certification (BS EN ISO 9000 or its equivalent), which may bring benefits with customers and suppliers or even be demanded by them.

9. Draw up your quality strategy

Use the results of the waste audit to draw up your quality strategy. This will cover:

- the goals of the strategy, including the revised mission
- the systems and tools needed to change processes
- the cultural changes needed to create the right environment for quality
- details of the resources that can be applied
- the time frames.

Secure senior management approval for the plan.

10. Draw up a management structure for change

The culture of the organisation will be critical to the success or failure of TQM. Plan for the introduction of team-based working: strong and effective teams are essential.

11. Establish an education and training programme

Some staff will need training in depth, others less so, but everyone should be given a thorough introduction to, and familiarisation with, what TQM means. Conduct an analysis of training needs in relation to TQM and cost the additional training required. This will need to be offset against the expected productivity gains. Plan for:

- general induction and training of all employees in the principles of TQM
- development of managers, supervisors and team leaders in the 'soft' skills needed to implement TQM
- job specific training in new techniques associated with TQM
- additional training in customer relations.

An external trainer or facilitator is almost always essential, especially in the early stages.

12. Opportunities and priorities for improvement

Set priorities for the introduction of TQM. Select key processes for early analysis and improvement. Do not start with more than three processes at the most. Choose at least one that is likely to demonstrate quick returns in business performance.

13. Goals and criteria for success

You will need to set both short- and long-term targets and establish measures of success both in business and cultural terms.

Dos and don'ts for mapping an effective TQM strategy

Do

- Secure top management commitment from the very beginning.
- Ensure that this commitment is repeatedly conveyed.
- Involve all employees in assessing current failures.

Don't

- See TQM as a quick fix.
- Bring TQM in at the same time as several other major new initiatives.
- Use TQM (or even appear to use TQM) as a means of downsizing.

Useful reading

How to lead your business beyond TQM: making world class performance a reality, Michael E Joyce, London: Pitman in association with the Financial Times, 1995
Managing quality, Desmond Bell, Philip McBride and George Wilson, Oxford: Butterworth Heinemann and the Institute of Management, 1994

Beyond total quality management, Larry Reynolds, London: Sheldon Press, 1994
Understanding total quality management in a week, John Macdonald, London: Hodder & Stoughton, 1998

Useful addresses

BSI Quality Assurance, 389 Chiswick High Road, London W4 4AL, Tel: 0181 996 9000
National Quality Information Centre, Institute of Quality Assurance, 10 Grosvenor Gardens, London SW1W 0DG, Tel: 0171 730 9986
Association of Quality Management Consultants, 4 Beyne Road, Olivers Battery, Winchester SO22 4JW, Tel: 01962 864394

Thought starters

- Is the climate really right for the introduction of TQM? In particular, do managers have the integrity and openness which TQM will demand of them?
- Does your strategy strike the right balance between the needs of your customer and those of your employees?

Total Quality: Getting TQM to Work

> This checklist provides guidance for those who have mapped a total quality management strategy for their organisation and are now seeking to implement it.

MCI Standards

This checklist has relevance for the MCI Management Standards: Key Role F – Manage Quality.

Definition

TQM is a way of managing which gives everyone in the organisation responsibility for delivering quality to the final customer; quality being described as 'fitness for purpose' or as 'delighting the customer'. TQM views each task in the organisation as fundamentally a process which is in a customer/supplier relationship with the next process. The aim at each stage is to define and meet the customer's requirements with the aim of maximising the satisfaction of the final consumer at the lowest possible cost.

Action checklist

1. Decide whether to run pilots

While you need to map a TQM strategy for the whole organisation, you will usually introduce it in stages. Select for the pilots areas or functions which are significant and where you feel TQM will yield results within a year at most: those will be critical in selling TQM to the sceptics.

2. Monitor and evaluate the results of the pilots

Draw up a framework and appoint a management team to assess and evaluate the results of the pilots. What lessons can be learned, and how can these be applied in introducing TQM elsewhere in the organisation?

3. Decide which tools and techniques to use at each of the four stages in the implementation of TQM

There are four key stages in the implementation of TQM: measurement; process management; problem solving and corrective action. For each, you need to select the tools and techniques appropriate to the scale and environment of your organisation.

4. Decide which measurement techniques to use

Measurement is critical to the success of TQM in quantifying situations and events and providing a benchmark by which to measure progress. The key is to ensure measurement is a meaningful process which leads to corrective action, rather than an end in itself. The main techniques are: measurement and error logging charts; corrective action systems; work process flow charts; run charts and process control charts.

5. Select process management tools

There is a battery of systems and tools to assist in process management. Many may already be used in the organisation for other purposes, including: Gantt charts, flow charts and histograms. Select those which are right for the culture of your organisation.

6. Set up mechanisms for problem solving

Plan to establish groups throughout the organisation to look at improving quality from different angles.

- Improvement groups are regular sessions led by supervisors of natural work groups.
- Key process groups analyse the operation of important processes.
- Innovation groups cross departments and are drawn from different levels within the organisation to look at totally new ways of working.

The groups have a range of techniques available to help them, including brainstorming, fishbone diagrams and Pareto analysis.

7. Set up corrective action mechanisms

The emphasis in TQM must be on identifying the causes of problems and solving them. Build in at the planning stage feedback loops with corrective action.

8. Draw up a communications plan for announcing the implementation across the organisation

Decide when and how to announce the programme. Assume that staff may initially be cynical or sceptical and work out strategies for overcoming this.

Use 'converts' from the pilots to explain the benefits. Make clear how TQM relates to other initiatives within the organisation.

9. Implement the education programme

Introduce the education programme mapped in your strategy. Target key groups first. Use these as the agents of change to cascade learning through the organisation.

10. Plan to create the right culture for quality

Successful TQM depends as much on cultural change as on process improvements. Be aware that TQM will probably need to be accompanied by a general programme of information and education targeted at employees, supervisors and managers.

11. Empower supervisors

The team leaders will be pivotal to the success of TQM. You need to give them the resources, time, support and education to become leaders.

12. Consider how to motivate employees to take ownership

Employees will need to take ownership of quality and act on their own initiative. To achieve this, you will need to create an open culture and drive out fears of failure, of taking risks and reprisals. You will also need to be prepared to deal with possible insecurities of managers who discover that all, or most, of their work is unnecessary or can be done by staff at lower levels.

13. Establish a programme of management change

Employees will not be able to make the changes needed without profound changes in management style. A new approach will be needed under TQM based on collaboration, consensus and participation: the largest single change for managers will be from telling to listening, from commanding to empowering.

14. Set short- and long-term goals for the implementation programme

Establish a means for monitoring progress. This will require a mix of short-term goals, to demonstrate progress, and more challenging long-term ones to stretch the organisation. Include a mix of business and cultural indicators.

15. Maintain the impetus

Culture changes will take a long time to show results but without results staff may be frustrated at what they can achieve through process improvements. Regularly review and report progress and recognise and publicise successes.

Dos and don'ts for the successful implementation of TQM

Do

- Make clear the relationship between TQM and other initiatives within the organisation.
- Work out where the invisible barriers to change are. Be aware of them from the outset and develop a strategy for overcoming them.
- Make clear that TQM is not a quick fix but an ongoing process of continuous improvement: you will never fully achieve total quality as the targets will constantly shift.
- Ensure that systems concentrate on measuring the performance of work processes rather than the individuals engaged in them.

Don't

- View TQM as a precisely defined methodology or a series of neatly tabled sequential actions to be completed one by one.
- Try to bring in TQM alongside other major initiatives if these already make heavy demands on management time.
- Neglect the soft side of TQM: changing culture is as important as changing processes.
- Lose sight of the ends by excessive concentration on the means.

Glossary of terms associated with TQM

Brainstorming is a simple approach used to help a group generate as many creative ideas as possible. Everyone is encouraged to speak and every idea is recorded without evaluation or criticism.

Corrective action depends on introducing management systems which require employees to identify the cause of a problem and remove it, so the problem does not recur, rather than just fixing the problem temporarily.

Fishbone charts, or **cause-and-effect diagrams,** explore in diagrammatic form the root causes of a problem.

Gantt charts are used in planning projects to show the proposed start and finish of each activity graphically against a common timetable.

Histograms are bar charts which show patterns of variation in different processes.

Pareto analysis is used to separate out and prioritise the significant items in a mass of data by applying to them the 80/20 rule: recording and analysis will usually show that 80% of the problems stem from 20% of the potential causes.

Process control or process flow charts are used to plot diagrammatically the sequence of events in a particular process.

Useful reading

Step change total quality: achieving world class business performance, Paul Spenley and Pera International, London: Chapman and Hall, 1995

Making TQM work, Kit Sadgrove, London: Kogan Page, 1995

Managing quality, Desmond Bell, Philip McBride and George Wilson, Oxford: Butterworth Heinemann and the Institute of Management, 1994

Understanding total quality management in a week, John Macdonald, London: Hodder & Stoughton, 1998

Useful addresses

British Standards Institution, 389 Chiswick High Road, London W4 4AL, Tel: 0181 996 7000

National Quality Information Centre, Institute of Quality Assurance, 10 Grosvenor Gardens, London SW1W 0DG, Tel: 0171 730 9986

Association of Quality Management Consultants, 4 Beyne Road, Olivers Battery, Winchester, SO22 4JW, Tel: 01962 864394

Thought starters

- Do you need to make changes to the structure of the organisation to make clear that quality is the responsibility of everyone?
- To what extent do current reward mechanisms promote employee involvement in quality?

Implementing Kaizen

This checklist is designed to introduce the concept of Kaizen and to explain its implementation.

In order to be successful, organisations are finding that they must continually improve their quality assurance, cost management and delivery systems. Equally, increasing competition has made it a priority for every organisation to develop and seek an advantage over rivals. A culture of continuous evaluation and improvement is seen by many organisations as an essential tool to achieve and maintain an advantage. Kaizen is one of the main tools to develop such a culture.

MCI Standards

This checklist has relevance for the MCI Management Standards: Key Roles A and F – Manage Activities and Manage Quality.

Definition

'Kaizen' is a Japanese term, which roughly translated means 'improvement'. 'Kai' means 'change' and 'zen' 'good' or 'for the better'. It means 'continuing improvement in personal life, home life, social life, and working life' (Imai, 1986). Essentially it means continuous improvement, seeking small improvements through the elimination of waste.

It is a philosophy which inspires the whole company with the instinct for improvement. The culture of seeking continuous improvement should involve everyone from the most senior manager to the most junior employee. Workers participate not for any particular financial reward, although these may be a part of the recognition process, but for the satisfaction of using their creative skills to improve the operations they perform and the goods and services they produce.

Kaizen incorporates a variety of techniques and principles into the overall culture and philosophy of improvement – improvement as a way of life, rather than the application of isolated techniques.

It can help build morale and self-respect in workers. The company benefits from a more motivated workforce, as well as improved financial returns resulting from more efficient operations. The customer benefits from the improved quality of product or service.

Advantages of implementing Kaizen

- All functions of the organisation come under continuous inspection.
- Employees most familiar with a particular operation on a day-to-day basis are the ones evaluating it.
- It serves to increase employee morale and job satisfaction.
- Waste is eliminated throughout the organisation, reducing costs and increasing efficiency.
- Product or service quality is improved and is monitored on a continuous basis.

Action checklist

1. Develop an understanding of the processes

According to Imai, there are three principal building-blocks, or keys to satisfying the customer, to be embraced under Kaizen:

- a continually improving quality assurance system to meet customer requirements
- a continually improving cost management system to provide the product or service at a favourable price to the customer
- a continually improving delivery system to meet customer requirements on time.

These are known collectively as QCD – quality, cost, delivery.

2. Identify corporate objectives

The three most important elements to creating the spirit of Kaizen are top management commitment, top management commitment and top management commitment. 'Without that, you had better forget the whole thing' (Imai).

Kaizen is best introduced as a means of achieving business targets. Senior managers and the board should carry out a SWOT analysis on the company's business programme. Existing systems and structures need to be assessed for their support for cross-functional goals and any necessary changes in terms of organisation, planning and control and personnel practices should be planned. Targets should be set for the next five years and commitment should be agreed and shared. A statement of commitment by senior management to such cross-functional goals as quality and cost, to the resourcing of the programme and to auditing its progress will demonstrate the commitment to Kaizen as a corporate strategy.

Kaizen is often introduced in organisations as a developmental step in total quality management. In such cases a culture of quality may have been achieved and quality is already part of all organisational planning. In order to move towards Kaizen, evaluate:

- how successful the quality initiative has been
- whether everybody understands the key importance of quality
- whether improvements made have been publicised
- employee attitudes towards quality.

3. Plan the Kaizen programme

A well-planned programme of Kaizen is often broken down into three segments – management-oriented, group-oriented and individual-oriented Kaizen, representing different levels of Kaizen.

- Management-oriented Kaizen focuses upon the most important strategic issues, processes and systems.
- Group-oriented Kaizen is based upon small-group activities that use statistical tools to solve problems.
- Individual-oriented Kaizen is based upon the assumption that each individual can work smarter and can contribute towards the improvement process.

Each segment requires particular consideration as it makes use of different management and personal skills.

4. Allocate resources

Senior management must be prepared to allocate resources. You need to appoint a director in overall charge of the project and a manager to implement the programme. Training will need to be introduced for all employees, and funding, as well as other resources, must be allocated to support this.

5. Develop a training plan

Explore the training requirements of your employees. An understanding of the continuous improvement process, of cross-functional working and of problem-solving techniques is a minimum requirement. Work with your training department or consultant to draw up a training plan.

6. Communicate with employees

Bring representatives from all functions and from all levels of the organisation into the planning process. Kaizen is about cultural change and employee participation, and ownership is an essential part of accepting the change process.

Arrange meetings, briefing sessions and newsletters to promote the objectives of Kaizen.

7. Focus training and development on the 4 Ps of quality

The four Ps are:

- Process control
  The management of processes to ensure a consistent and reliable level of performance.
  - Identify variations and their causes.
  - Deal with assignable causes.
  - Deal with random variation.
  - Undertake process design reviews, making use as necessary of the range of analytical and quality improvement techniques – flowcharts, cause-and-effect (or fishbone) diagrams, process models, audits and process capability studies.
- Problem identification
  Failure to understand the causes of process variation gives rise to incorrect identification of problems. Consider using a range of techniques (quality systems audits, customer complaint analysis, cost of quality studies, benchmarking, departmental purpose analysis and customer and employee surveys) to identify problems.
- Problem elimination
  Gain an understanding of problem-solving tools (Pareto diagrams, cause-and-effect diagrams, histograms, control charts and scatter diagrams). Test solutions to see that they work, truly prevent the problem and do not cause new trouble elsewhere. Implement the solution after gaining an understanding of the dynamics of change.
- Permanence
  Improvement is a continuous process. You need to ensure that the changes already made stick and that you go on improving. The use of processes such as policy deployment, TQM reviews and quality function deployment is suggested. Ensuring that senior managers regularly attend quality improvement group meetings maintains momentum and commitment.

8. Set up a suggestion scheme

Involving employees is an integral part of individual-oriented Kaizen. A suggestion scheme is a good way of encouraging employee contribution. Be prepared to listen to all suggestions. Give recognition to employees' efforts and offer awards based on predetermined criteria.

9. Review

Plan to review the development of the Kaizen programme. Assess the extent to which a process-oriented culture change has been achieved. Recognise champions and consider further training as required.

Dos and don'ts for implementing Kaizen

Do

- Gain the commitment of senior management.
- Involve everybody in the organisation.
- Acknowledge that all organisations have problems.
- View the introduction of Kaizen as a cultural change process.

Don't

- Forget that the search for improvement is never ending.

Useful reading

BOOKS

Kaizen. The key to Japan's competitive success, Masaaki Imai, New York: Random House, 1986

TQM in action: a practical approach to continuous performance improvement, John Pike and Richard Barnes, London: Chapman and Hall, 1994

JOURNAL ARTICLE

Kaizen – changing for the better, Masaaki Imai, Director, July 1993, pp15-16

Useful address

Kaizen Institute, 4 Tavistock Place, London WC1H 9RA, Tel: 0171 713 0407

Thought starters

- Can you afford not to be interested in improved quality and greater productivity?
- Are you making full use of the creative ability of all your employees?
- Do you use the full range of problem-solving techniques?

Preparing for ISO 9000

This checklist is for managers involved with the implementation of ISO 9000 within their organisation, and details the steps and processes involved.

Most quality drives are aimed at customer satisfaction and many elements are involved in this process. These include training, 'getting it right first time', empowerment, performance measurement and managing change. ISO 9000 obliges you to design a model or quality system to create order from a bundle of initiatives which might otherwise create more problems than they solve. Achieving ISO 9000 gives accreditation to an internationally recognised standard.

MCI Standards

This checklist has relevance for the MCI Management Standards: Key Role F – Manage Quality.

Definition

ISO 9000 acts as a framework to allow an organisation to develop a quality system which suits its own way of working. It lays down a general set of principles about good management practice which identifies the basic disciplines and specifies the criteria and procedures to ensure that products and services meet customers' requirements. It also provides a framework for measuring the consistency of an organisation's systems for dealing with customer orders, purchasing, stock control, service provision and service delivery.

Advantages of ISO 9000

- Provides consistency in the organisation's response to customers.
- Gives the customer confidence that the intended quality is being delivered.
- Improves communication by talking about what you do and how you do it.
- Clarifies tasks so that everyone knows what they are doing and how.
- Generates a training and reference manual.
- Aids the pursuit of value for money from suppliers.
- Sets a target to aim for in a quality programme.
- Gives you a recognised cachet.

Disadvantages of ISO 9000

- Time consuming.
- Costly (but so is the cost of getting things wrong).
- Staff often need convincing that it is not just a bureaucratic process.

Action checklist

1. Buy and read the standard and relevant guidelines

There are three major alternative parts to ISO 9000. Choose the one which is most appropriate for your organisation. The language of the standard betrays its origins in the manufacturing and defence industries, but guidelines are available for service industries to help interpret the standard in their environment.

2. Gain top management commitment

The standard places the responsibility on management to establish, document and communicate a quality policy. Therefore, senior management commitment is vital and should be visible. This could be achieved, for example, by the chief executive signing the policy statement, holding briefing meetings or authorising the display of posters with the quality message.

3. Decide whether the whole, or just part, of the organisation should become registered

It is possible for one or more departments (termed 'clusters' in the language of the standard) to apply for registration if it is not appropriate for the whole organisation.

4. Appoint a quality manager and choose a registration body

The management representative, often referred to as the quality manager, has overall day-to-day responsibility for the quality system. This person must be a member of the organisation's own staff, not an outside consultant. The quality manager's first job will be to select a registration body. Check with the National Accreditation Council for Certification Bodies (NACCB) that your choice of registration body has the registered scope to assess your organisation.

5. Decide whether to hire a consultant

Depending on the resources and expertise available in the organisation you may need to employ a consultant. A consultant can add value in terms of helping to interpret and apply the requirements to your own situation, but does not remove the importance of the ownership and involvement of staff.

Employing a consultant will certainly add to the cost of achieving ISO 9000.

6. Involve staff

This is a critical area for managers where they need to employ all the techniques of managing change. The first task is to gain the commitment of staff by showing your belief in the benefits of the standard and dispelling some of the myths that have mushroomed around it – for example, 'it's not about quality'. (Although ISO 9000 does not test the quality of the final product or service, if the standard is applied properly then quality systems will improve, and so will the delivery of the final product or service).

7. Interpret the requirements

There are twenty requirements in the standard, which can be grouped according to their management or operational nature.

Management/macro requirements	Operational requirements
1. Management responsibility	4. Designing
2. Quality system	6. Purchasing
3. Contract review	7. Control of customer-supplied product
5. Document control	8. Product identification and traceability
17. Internal quality audit	9. Process control
18. Training	10. Inspection and testing
	11. Inspection, measuring and test equipment
	12. Inspection and test runs
	13. Control of non-conforming product
	14. Corrective and preventative action
	15. Handling, storage, packaging, preservation and delivery
	16. Quality records
	19. Servicing
	20. Statistical techniques

Some of the requirements will be easier to apply than others, some will be less relevant (particularly in service organisations), some may be already in place and some will require a great deal of thought and interpretation. You must demonstrate that even if a requirement is irrelevant, you have at least considered it carefully.

8. Draw up a quality plan

The quality plan describes the practices, resources and sequence of activities relevant to a particular organisation or department. Although a quality plan is not mandatory, it can be very useful in identifying the main areas of activity and their associated tasks. It will help you work out how they fit or relate to the standard's requirements. In order to do this, it is helpful if the quality plan takes the form of a flow chart showing, for example, your operation from the purchasing through to the customer delivery stage.

9. Write and apply the procedures

The fifth requirement of the standard relates to document control. This is a key area for staff involvement. It is important that they work out what needs to be documented and take part in the writing of procedures. Remember that although you decide what to include or exclude, a collection of written procedures can form a valuable training document. The key objective in using procedures is for everyone to do what they have agreed to do. Another message to communicate is that procedures can be changed – in fact the certification body will check that the system is dynamic and not cast in stone.

10. Establish performance indicators

A framework must be established to assess and agree with your customers what they want, bearing in mind the resources you have and the objectives to which you are working. You then need to measure how well you are doing, how realistic the indicators are and whether there is room for improvement.

11. Audit with a dummy run

An initial review prior to full assessment is advisable. This provides the quality manager and a representative from the certification body with the opportunity to check that staff do what the procedures say they do, and that you have covered all the requirements of the standard.

12. Test and implement corrective procedures

An auditor will always find something amiss. If it is major (such as not meeting the requirements) then it could affect registration, as it means that something in the overall system has gone badly wrong. If it is minor, the auditor will issue a Corrective Action Notice which the staff representative will agree. Then either change the procedure, or what is done, or both, and ensure that the new practice is documented for all who need to know.

13. Get ready for assessment

The assessment proper has two parts: the documentation audit and the implementation audit. In the former the assessor will look for a quality system which addresses all the requirements of the standard, and in the latter the assessing team will look for evidence that what has been committed to paper is actually being done. This means that the system should have been operational for at least 4-5 months prior to assessment.

Once you are awarded ISO 9000 registration, it is important to check that your procedures are kept up-to-date and continue to be met. An external assessor will visit annually to ensure that this is the case.

Standards

BS EN ISO9001: 1994. Quality systems: model for quality assurance in design, development, production, installation and servicing

BS EN ISO9002: 1994. Quality systems: model for quality assurance in production, installation and servicing

BS EN ISO9003: 1994. Quality systems: model for quality assurance in final inspection and test

BS 5750 Part 4: 1994. Quality systems: guide to the use of BS EN ISO9001/2/3

Dos and don'ts for ISO 9000 accreditation

Do
- Focus on the customer.
- Read the standard.
- Involve staff.
- Keep procedures simple.
- What you say you do.

Don't
- Write all the procedures yourself.
- Strait-jacket procedures so they are not flexible enough.
- Load procedures with unnecessary detail.
- Be afraid to change procedures.

Useful reading

Achieving the new international quality standards: a step by step guide to BS EN ISO 9000, Lesley Munro-Faure, Malcolm Munro-Faure and Edward Bones, London: Pitman, 1995

Gaining and benefiting from ISO 9000 registration: a step by step guide, M J Fox, Cheltenham: Stanley Thornes, 1994

ISO 9000 quality systems handbook, 2nd ed, David Hoyle, Oxford: Butterworth Heinemann, 1994

Useful addresses

British Standards Institution (BSI), 389 Chiswick High Road, London W4 4AL. Orders – Publications Tel: 0181 996 7000. Information Tel: 0181 996 7111

The National Accreditation Council for Certification Bodies (NACCB), Audley House, 13 Palace Street, London SW1E 5HS, Tel: 0171 233 7111

Thought starters

The following questions will help you judge the potential usefulness of ISO 9000:

- How do you know what the customer wants?
- How much repeat business do you get?
- How consistent is the response given to customers?
- How do you know if your suppliers' performance is satisfactory?

Setting Up a Customer Care Programme

This checklist describes the stages in establishing an organisational framework that maximises the value offered to and derived from customers.

MCI Standards

This checklist has relevance for the MCI Management Standards: Key Roles A and G – Manage Activities and Manage Projects.

Definition

Successful customer care means making the customer want to come back for more, and getting them to recommend products and services to others. Customer care is not only about meeting customer expectations but 'delighting' the customer by focusing staff energies on offering value, getting it right first time, and yet improving it in the future.

Benefits of a customer care programme

A comprehensive customer care programme impacts on the organisation through:

● increased success
● a developing and satisfied workforce.

Drawbacks of a customer care programme

There can be no such thing as a zero customer care programme – to take no account of customers is to ignore the future of the business.

Action checklist

1. Secure top management commitment

Unless top management are fully committed to the concept of customer care, there is very little chance of success. A formalised customer care programme with involved leadership helps to focus roles and responsibilities in a clear manner.

2. Know your customers

Excellence in customer care is wholly reliant upon knowing your customers' needs and expectations. Needs are not the same as demands: people don't ask for what they don't expect to get, even when it could be provided. Anticipating real needs can give competitive advantage.

While it is important to remember that most organisations have internal customers in other departments, divisions and sectors, establishing external customers' needs can be a lot more complex. A range of approaches is available, including:

- feedback direct from customers and staff
- direct discussion with customers
- analysis of customer complaints, enquiries and thank-yous
- attitude surveys and questionnaires
- visits to premises
- focus-group discussions and customer audits.

3. Assimilate the major elements of customer care

Customer care is more than just an excellent product or a first-class service; it involves a host of elements that contribute to genuine care and value for the customer, such as, in the purchasing process:

- clarity of literature on product features, price, payment methods, availability and after-sales support
- the way the first contact takes place and is followed up
- simple ordering procedures highlighted by convenience for the customer
- prompt order processing
- prompt notification of any changes to specification or procedure
- clear invoicing with no hidden charges
- assistance when the product is delivered
- easy after-sales contacts.

4. Develop service levels

It may be the case that performance standards do exist but are not formalised, recorded or audited. It is not good enough to set indicators or levels which place supplier-convenience in front of customer-convenience; such levels should be worked out, discussed and agreed with customers. It is good to set levels which are challenging but have a realistic chance of attainment. Questions to help set service levels may include:

- How many times does the phone ring before someone answers?
- How many transfers take place before the customer gets an answer?
- How long does it take to process an order?
- How long does it take to respond to a complaint?

Measurements must not gain such a hold on processes that they become a time-consuming nuisance; they should be realistic and helpful in developing a relationship – however short-lived – between supplier and customer. Remember, what gets measured, gets done.

5. Recruit the right staff

Your service is only as professional as the people delivering it; attracting new customers and retaining existing ones are tasks for competent people. Focusing the recruitment process on customer care can mean introducing questions at the interview stage, covering, for example:

- candidates' experiences with customers
- service levels and customer expectations
- the prioritisation of customer needs over in-house organisational activities
- incentives to motivate front-line staff.

Remember to include customer care on the induction programme.

6. Get your communications right

Top management commitment to a customer care programme is no good if the right message is not conveyed to all staff in the right way. If internal communications are not working as well as they should, then external communications cannot be expected to be successful. Communications have to be reliable, consistent and regular so that all people receive the same message and interpret it in the same way so that the end results are the same.

7. Convert complainants back into customers

Prompt and sympathetic handling of complaints can turn a disgruntled customer into a happy – and longer-lasting – one. People whose complaints are fully dealt with are more loyal than those who have no complaints.

Often, those who receive the complaint are not at fault, yet they bear the brunt of customer dissatisfaction. It is vital that all staff are familiar and comfortable with the organisation's procedure so that they are prepared to receive complaints and to start converting the customer from dissatisfied to satisfied. Remembering that the complaint must be dealt with promptly, accurately – it may just be a misunderstanding or lack of information – and efficiently, individuals in the 'front line' need to be familiar with seven rules for dealing with verbal complaints:

- Listen patiently – let the customer air the grievance without interruption.
- Acknowledge the customer's viewpoint – even if you don't agree.
- Apologise – say sorry if a mistake has been made, but there's no need to overdo it.
- Find a solution – establish what needs to be done to rectify the problem.
- Keep the complainant informed – lack of ongoing information can exacerbate the problem.
- Reach a conclusion to resolve the problem for the customer quickly – a more permanent solution may take longer to find.
- Follow up – check that promised action happens.

8. Reward service accomplishments

Recognition and reward for superior performance helps with reinforcement. Try to recognise smaller accomplishments not just the major ones.

Customers too appreciate rewards for their loyalty, and such rewards will make a significant contribution to their retention.

9. Stay close to your customers

Staying close to customers means:

- carrying out continuous research in order to learn from them
- asking questions about the quality and performance of the product at regular intervals after the sale
- developing procedures to stay up-to-date with customer needs
- listening.

10. Train your people and work towards continuous improvement

Recruiting the right staff is just one of the first steps in a customer care programme. Training staff to understand customer needs and tackle customer problems, to turn threats into opportunities for the organisation, is also a prerequisite for effective and lasting customer care. Training them on a continuing basis, especially in friendly telephone and face-to-face techniques, which result in sincerity and substance rather than empty phraseology, can provide organisations with an advantage that will score with customers.

Providing feedback from customers is especially motivating for staff in 'backrooms', who are not in direct contact with customers. Feedback can make an important contribution to continuous improvements in not only how things are done but also what is done.

Dos and don'ts for setting up a customer care programme

Do

- Make recruitment and selection customer-oriented activities.
- Discuss customer levels of expectation with all staff.
- Analyse complaints to discern any trends or patterns.
- Offer incentives to encourage customers to give feedback.
- Stay close to your customers – the profile of your best prospect is the profile of your best customer.

Don't

- Forget to involve all staff in customer service discussions.
- Lose sight of your internal customers.
- Neglect to celebrate and publicise good news and achievements.
- Omit to record thanks as well as complaints.
- Say 'It isn't my fault', or 'I don't know who deals with that here'.

Useful reading

Successful customer care in a week, John Wellemin, London: Hodder & Stoughton, 1995

Creating a customer focused company: 25 proven customer strategies, Ian Linton, London: Pitman, 1994

Perfect customer care, Ted Johns, London: Arrow, 1994

Raising the standard: a survey of managers' attitudes to customer care, Neville Benbow, Corby: Institute of Management, 1994

Keeping customers for life, Richard F Gerson, London: Kogan Page, 1992

Thought starters

- A service that receives no complaints may receive little else – a service that ignores complaints will receive less use.
- What irritates you as a customer of other organisations? What delights you?
- How can you:
    - improve ordering/purchasing convenience for your customers?
    - develop more direct relationships with your customers?
    - reward loyal customers?
    - recognise customer (dis)satisfaction?

Handling Complaints

This checklist outlines a procedure for handling complaints in small or large, manufacturing or service, private or public sector organisations.

It is designed to enable a consistent organisation-wide approach to complaints which ensures that they are dealt with effectively to the advantage of both the customer and the organisation.

MCI Standards

This checklist has relevance for the MCI Management Standards: Key Role A – Manage Activities.

Definition

A complaint is an expression of lack of satisfaction with any product or service, whether orally or in writing, from an internal or external customer.

Advantages

A complaints procedure:

- provides a clear approach when a complaint occurs
- engenders understanding and confidence on how to tackle complaints
- helps to remove personal 'guilt' feelings when receiving a complaint
- leads to a recognition of complaints as valuable feedback, not criticisms
- can produce records for analysing possible service improvements.

Action checklist

1. Establish a common approach to handling complaints

This must have widespread approval from the top to the bottom of the organisation, including staff who do not come into direct contact with customers. Ensure that everyone is thinking about customers in the same way. This should be embedded into the organisation's culture and is primarily the responsibility of senior management.

Remember that when customers complain, they like to be:

- aware of who is dealing with the complaint
- listened to and believed
- treated fairly and efficiently
- kept informed of progress
- compensated if it is appropriate.

2. Draw up a standard complaints form

This is a valuable tool which should include the following sub-headings:

Receipt details
- date received
- received by
- department/division

Customer details
- name, address, identifier
- telephone / fax / e-mail

Complaint details

Action (to be) taken
- date completed
- sign-off
- line superior.

3. Ensure complaints are assessed correctly

On receipt of a complaint, the recipient should look on it as a second chance to satisfy the customer. Staff should:

- be courteous and empathise with the customer
- ensure that all the details are obtained and recorded on the standard complaints form
- be satisfied that the information is factual
- not admit liability or fault at this stage.

Subject to appropriate information seeking and establishment of the facts, the recipient, in conjunction with his or her line manager if necessary, should decide whether it is a major or minor complaint.

Minor complaints may result from misinterpretation, misunderstanding, detail errors, or straightforward carelessness. Major complaints may involve breach of the criminal law or have health and safety or financial implications.

4. Establish ownership and responsibility

Staff should be empowered to take appropriate action if the complaint is clearly justified, falls within their jurisdiction, and can be rectified immediately. If the complaint cannot be resolved by the recipient, details of the customer and complaint should be noted on the form and passed quickly to the relevant area or level of responsibility. The customer should be told who is dealing with the complaint – nothing is more frustrating than dealing with a faceless organisation, or being passed from one person to another – and that a reply will be given as soon as possible, and within a specified time limit.

5. Establish escalation procedures

In the case of major complaints, the manager should decide on the appropriate action and this may involve:

- consulting a higher authority
- the production of a detailed report on the events
- contact with the organisation's solicitor
- contact with the police.

6. Emphasise customer contact for complaint resolution

If the level of seriousness has been properly understood, and the establishment of the facts correctly carried out, then appropriate action should become apparent. Problem resolution is not a time for negotiation or bartering with a customer who has a genuine grievance and who should perhaps be compensated generously. If there is any delay in resolving complaints, the customer should be contacted at regular, agreed intervals so that a progress update can be given.

7. Ensure complaints forms are signed off

When the problem has been resolved to the satisfaction of the customer, the recipient or superior should sign off the complaints form for subsequent analysis of any complaints trends.

It could be that there is no satisfactory solution, that the customer may require something 'unreasonable' or 'beyond' the remit of the organisation to deliver. If this occurs, it may be appropriate to:

- inform the customer that expectations exceeded capabilities
- re-affirm which steps can be taken
- and to state that a report will be passed on to senior management.

8. Decide internal corrective action

Having dealt with the complaint, decide whether any system, equipment or personnel-related improvement needs tackling. Deal with internal process improvements or training requirements as soon as possible after the complaint has occurred.

9. Build in customer satisfaction checks

After an appropriate interval, say two weeks, get back in touch with the customer to confirm that the complaint was satisfactorily resolved – and to check that the organisation still has a customer.

10. Analyse complaints periodically

All complaints forms should be returned to a simple, central address where a manager should have responsibility for monitoring the level and nature of complaints on a regular basis. The results of this analysis, and details of any corrective action, should be reported to senior management on a regular basis.

Dos and don'ts for handling complaints

Do
- Make customer service part of the corporate culture.
- Empower staff to deal with complaints.
- Keep in contact with the customer to ensure that the complaint is dealt with to their satisfaction.
- Analyse the pattern of complaints and take action to make improvements.
- Treat complaints positively.

Courtesy, speed of response and a personal touch are essential. A complaining customer who gets all three will usually emerge a more satisfied customer than before he/she had any complaints. And he/she will tell others in turn.

Don't allow staff to:
- blame the computer
- say it's not their department
- take the complaint personally or defensively
- allocate blame
- use paperwork to block a fast response to complaints.

Offhandedness, slowness and impersonality are likely to lose you not only that customer but many others as well – bad news spreads.

Useful reading

Successful customer care in a week, John Wellemin, London: Hodder & Stoughton, 1995

Creating a customer focused company: 25 proven customer strategies, Ian Linton, London: Pitman, 1994

Perfect customer care, Ted Johns, London: Arrow, 1994

Raising the standard: a survey of managers' attitudes to customer care, Neville Benbow, Corby: Institute of Management, 1994

Keeping customers for life, Richard F Gerson, London: Kogan Page, 1992

Thought starters

- Do staff know what to do when they receive a complaint?
- Does the organisation receive many complaints?
- Does it receive many different kinds of complaints?
- Are they recorded?
- What happens to the records?
- When you last complained, how was it dealt with? Have you used that organisation again?
- An organisation that never has any complaints is probably a bad one – no one bothers to complain, they just go elsewhere.

Further *Business Checklists* titles from Hodder & Stoughton and the
Institute of Management all at £8.99

0 340 74292 5	Information & Financial Management	❏
0 340 74290 9	Marketing & Strategy	❏
0 340 74288 7	People Management	❏
0 340 74294 1	Personal Effectiveness & Career Development	❏
0 340 74289 5	Personnel Policies, Training & Development	❏
0 340 74293 3	Small Business Management	❏

*All Hodder & Stoughton books are available from your local bookshop or
can be ordered direct from the publisher. Just tick the titles you want and fill
in the form below. Prices and availability subject to change without notice.*

To: Hodder & Stoughton Ltd, Cash Sales Department, Bookpoint, 78
Milton Park, Abingdon, Oxon OX14 4TD. If you have a credit card you
may order by telephone – 01235 400414
                              fax – 01235 400454
E-mail address: orders@bookpoint.co.uk

Please enclose a cheque or postal order made payable to Bookpoint Ltd to the
value of the cover price and allow the following for postage and packaging:

UK & BFPO: £4.30 for one book; £6.30 for two books; £8.30 for three
books.

OVERSEAS & EIRE: £4.80 for one book; £7.10 for 2 or 3 books (surface
mail).

Name: ....

Address: ....

....

....

If you would prefer to pay by credit card, please complete:

Please debit my Visa/Mastercard/Diner's Card/American Express (delete as
appropriate) card no:

❏ ❏ ❏ ❏ ❏ ❏ ❏ ❏ ❏ ❏ ❏ ❏ ❏ ❏ ❏ ❏

Signature .... Expiry date ....